Louis Dudek & Raymond Souster

STUDIES IN
CANADIAN LITERATURE

CHAMPLAIN COLLEGE

Louis Dudek & Raymond Souster

Frank Davey

Douglas & McIntyre
VANCOUVER

This book has been published with the help of a grant from the Canadian Federation for the Humanities, using funds provided by the Social Sciences and Humanities Research Council of Canada.

Douglas & McIntyre Ltd.
1615 Venables Street
Vancouver, British Columbia

Canadian Cataloguing in Publication Data

Davey, Frank, 1940
    Louis Dudek & Raymond Souster
    (Studies in Canadian Literature)

    Bibliography: p.
    ISBN 0-88894-264-8

    1.Dudek, Louis, 1918–   –Criticism and interpretation.· 2. Souster, Raymond, 1921–
    –Criticism and interpretation.   I. Title.
II. Series.
PS8507.U34Z63   C811'.54   C80-091215-2
PR9199.3.D83Z63

Typesetting by The Typeworks, Mayne Island
Cover design by Nancy Legue
Printed and bound in Canada by D.W. Friesen & Sons Ltd.

Contents

Abbreviations   vi
One / Editors and Publishers   1
Two / Functional Poetry   38
Three / Europe, En México, Atlantis   53
Four / The Red Truck   82
Five / Get the Poem Outdoors   102
Six / The Penny Flute   123
Seven / A Long-Lost World   138
Eight / Canadian Modernists   159
Notes   176
Bibliography   191
Acknowledgements   199

Abbreviations

Passages from the works of Dudek and Souster are in the following editions.

By Louis Dudek

A   *Atlantis*.   Montreal: Delta Canada, 1967.

CP   *Collected Poetry*.   Montreal: Delta Canada, 1971.

D/k   *D/k. Some Letters of Ezra Pound*.   Montreal: DC Books, 1974.

EC   *East of the City*.   Toronto: Ryerson Press, 1946.

EM   *En México*.   Toronto: Contact Press, 1958.

Ep   *Epigrams*.   Montreal: DC Books, 1975.

E   *Europe*.   Toronto: Lacoon (Contact) Press, 1954.

FPL   *The First Person in Literature*.   Toronto: CBC Publications, 1967.

LS   *Laughing Stalks*.   Toronto: Contact Press, 1958.

LP   *Literature and the Press*.   Toronto: Ryerson/ Contact Press, 1960.

SEC   *Selected Essays and Criticism*.   Ottawa: Tecumseh Press, 1978.

SI   *The Searching Image*.   Toronto: Ryerson Press, 1952.

TS   *The Transparent Sea*. Toronto: Contact Press, 1956.

TP   *Twenty-four Poems*. Toronto: Contact Press, 1952.

By Raymond Souster

AI   *As Is*. Toronto: Oxford University Press, 1967.

ALP   *A Local Pride*. Toronto: Contact Press, 1962.

C   *Cerberus* (Louis Dudek, Irving Layton, Raymond Souster). Toronto: Contact Press, 1952.

CU   *Change-up*. Ottawa: Oberon Press, 1974.

CT   *The Colour of the Times*. Toronto: Ryerson Press, 1964.

EI   *Extra Innings*. Ottawa: Oberon Press, 1977.

GTSW   *Go To Sleep, World*. Toronto: Ryerson Press, 1947.

L&F   *Lost & Found*. Toronto: Clarke Irwin, 1968.

OT   *On Target* (by John Holmes, pseud.). Toronto: Village Book Store Press, 1972.

PM   *Place of Meeting*. Toronto: Gallery Editions, [1962].

SP   *Selected Poems*. Ottawa: Oberon Press, 1972.

SFSG   *So Far So Good*. Ottawa: Oberon Press, 1969.

TEYS   *Ten Elephants on Yonge Street*. Toronto: Ryerson Press, 1965.

TSP   *The Selected Poems*. Toronto: Contact Press, 1956.

WWAY   *When We Are Young*. Montreal: First Statement Press, [1946].

Y   *The Years*. Ottawa: Oberon Press, 1971.

CHAPTER ONE

Editors and Publishers

Louis Dudek and Raymond Souster first met in 1943, as dinner guests of John Sutherland at a Montreal restaurant. Souster, en route by train from his Royal Canadian Air Force base at Sydney, Nova Scotia, to his parents' home in Toronto, had "suddenly appeared"[1] that day at Sutherland's apartment. Eager to talk with Sutherland, who had just launched the crusading new literary magazine *First Statement* and who had recently accepted him as a contributor, Souster found Dudek's merely one of a number of new faces that punctuated his nightlong discussions and arguments with Sutherland. Yet within two decades his friendship with Dudek would have shaped various literary magazines, founded an important small press, and modified the direction of their nation's literature.

There was little in their backgrounds to suggest the possibility of an association between Dudek and Souster. Souster had been born in 1921 into a lower middleclass Toronto family, and one of his favourite activities in childhood had been pitching in bantam and juvenile baseball leagues. After graduation from high school in 1939 he had followed his father into a banking career[2] which he had interrupted in 1941 to enlist as a tradesman in the RCAF.[3] Dudek had been born in Montreal in 1918 to Roman Catholic parents who had emigrated only the previous year from Poland. He had been educated in Montreal's Protestant English-language school system because his father believed that the Protestant system offered a better education. Dudek had enrolled in 1936 at McGill University and completed a B.A. in English and History in 1939. He had been active in the "No Conscription League" in the early 1940s; at the time of the 1943 meeting with Souster he was employed by the Canadian Advertising Agency[4] and was seriously considering enrolling at Columbia University for graduate study in journalism and history.

However, although their training and family backgrounds were different, the academically trained Dudek and Leading Aircraftsman Souster did share a belief in themselves as potential poets and strong feelings of estrangement from bourgeois society, from conventional poetics and from recognized literary circles. They both had strong inclinations towards aggressive and rebellious literary action. Some of their feelings of estrangement from the literary "establishment" were undoubtedly due to youthful iconoclasm and some to the real and seemingly insurmountable difficulties then faced by young writers trying to get their work into print. Dudek's antagonism seems also to have been a result of the isolation of the Polish community in Montreal and of the year of unemployment he suffered following graduation from McGill; Souster's alienation seems to have been partly a result of his awareness of the injustices of the Depression years, manifest to him most clearly in his and his father's salaries as bank clerks. In their writings at this time, both Souster and Dudek expressed hostility towards the older writers who enjoyed what acclaim and publication were then available to a Canadian writer, and both were angry and impatient with the way in which limited publication opportunities were retarding growth and change within Canadian literature. In 1943, Dudek contributed two rather Marxist articles to *First Statement*: "Geography, Politics, and Poetry" and "Academic Literature." The first was an attack on " 'upper class,' hybrid-cultured, intellectual spirit"[5] in poetry, and the second a somewhat gentler assault on A.J.M. Smith's newly published anthology, *The Book of Canadian Poetry,* and on the "blue-blood artist" who writes "word patterns rather than poetry."[6] Later, in 1943, Souster assailed the Canadian Authors' Association and the "Sir Charles G.D. tradition," and in discussions with William Goldberg and David Mullen towards founding their own literary magazine, *Direction*, at his air base at Sydney, declared: "We must attack, attack, and attack. Let us call the mag the Attack or Sperm, anything which will shock the dull witted Canadian imagination out of its lethargy."[7]

In retrospect, it seems appropriate that Souster and Dudek should meet in the presence of John Sutherland. All the characteristics Souster and Dudek had in common—convictions of their poetic talent, deep feelings of social and literary estrangement, a yearning to commit literary rebellion—Sutherland shared. Although a year younger than Dudek and only two years older than Souster, he was already through his editorship of *First Statement* forcing Canadian letters to accommodate him. Both Souster and Dudek appear to have been fascinated by the example of Sutherland's commitment, his literary methods and his publication techniques. Both perceived the relevance of Sutherland's iconoclasm to their hopes for their own work and for Canadian poetry; more importantly, both recognized that Sutherland's use of the "little magazine" form had deeply interwoven sociological and literary implications. Dudek would later decide to study the sociology of literature at Columbia University; Souster, within a few months of meeting Sutherland and Dudek, would launch from within the RCAF the little magazine *Direction*—a magazine designed as an "enema"[8] for the Canadian literary establishment and as a mild attack on war.

The careers of Dudek and Souster have an enormous debt to the early work of Sutherland. In fact, because of Sutherland's conversion to Catholicism in 1954 and his unexpected embrace of conservative literary ideas during 1950–51, their activities eventually formed a more consistent extension of much of that work than does the later career of Sutherland himself. It is therefore important to note the values, goals and methods of Sutherland's early publishing ventures. *First*

Statement appears to have been conceived by him in 1942 as an alternative to the "elitism" of Patrick Anderson's magazine, *Preview*, founded earlier that year. In his second editorial, Sutherland declared his interest in a general audience: "Almost everyone is a potential critic of this magazine. Almost everyone would have plenty to say if the magazine ever came to his attention. . . . " He also stated, in an almost apocalyptic tone, his intention of making *First Statement* an embodiment of the hope of youth.

> The religious ceremonies which thrived many centuries ago must have arisen from a belief in the newness of living and the youth of the race. What had happened seemed rare, and it was not certain that it would happen again. Bread was broken to express the hope that bread would be granted again. We intend to go through the ceremonies, in our Canadian literary youth.[9]

Sutherland's early editorial policies were eclectic. He intended "to exhibit . . . the various types of writing as we find them in Canada."[10] Five months later, however, after he had established literary friendships with Dudek, Souster and Irving Layton and they had become contributors to *First Statement*, the magazine began to react not only against *Preview* but also against the first wave of modernism in Canadian poetry.[11] This first wave had been inspired by the earliest work of Anglo-American modernists such as Pound, Hulme and Wyndham Lewis, by their calls for a time-transcending poetry "as much like granite as it can be"[12] and for "forms which can almost be called geometrical."[13] Beginning in 1926, modernism's chief proponent in Canada was A.J.M. Smith; he was later joined in his support for "pure poetry . . . objective, impersonal . . . timeless and absolute"[14] by Ralph Gustafson, Robert Finch, P.K. Page and Patrick Anderson. After the first few issues, *First Statement* began to espouse something quite different, not a "search after an austerity, a *perfection* and rigidity which vital things can never have,"[15] but the values of an evolved modernism that embraced Spender, Auden, Hart Crane, Kenneth Fearing, Dylan Thomas, Marianne Moore and E.E. Cummings. The new magazine showed a growing commitment to the temporal, phenomenal world, to "fundamental realism,"[16] use of the natural speaking voice, attention to local experience as a source of subject matter, and especially to the breaking down of "the dividing wall between the author and the people," to ensuring that "poetry is coming into contact with the . . . environment."[17] *First Statement* challenged the elitist and "cosmopolitan" values of A.J.M. Smith (to Sutherland, "Bishop Smith") and argued that his preference for Eliotic impersonality, detachment and "intelligence" and his ideal of a "civilized" and "international" style encouraged writing that was both obscure and "colonial"; the cosmopolitan or international style was to Sutherland something established in England and superimposed on Canadian experience by poets such as Smith. Speaking of the poetry of James Wreford, Ronald Hambleton, P.K. Page and Patrick Anderson, Sutherland declared:

> our poetry is colonial because it is the product of a cultured English group who are out of touch with a people who long ago began adjusting themselves to life on this continent.[18]

Dudek's account of the "opposition" between *First Statement* and *Preview* emphasizes *First Statement*'s rejection of colonialism and its championing of North American models:

> that's the crucial thing about it, that one magazine, *Preview*, was associated with what I think of, historically, as the colonial attachment of Canadian literature: their poetry had affinities with the English poetry of the preceding decade — especially Auden and Thomas, whereas the *First Statement* people were more related to contemporary American poetry, Twentieth-century American poetry stemming out of Walt Whitman — Carl Sandburg, William Carlos Williams, and eventually Ezra Pound. And therefore what you had in these two magazines was a significant confrontation between the colonial pull toward British literature and the new native strain that would come right out of Canada.[19]

Throughout its early issues, *First Statement* affirmed hope for Canadian poetry. It examined both the history and contemporary politics of Canadian literature. Souster and Dudek undoubtedly owed to *First Statement* much of their appreciation of Canadian literature and its potential for growth.

Sutherland ran both *First Statement* and First Statement Press with stringent economy. He was careful not to over-extend his energy or his finances and made no unnecessary concessions to format or regular publication schedules. He seems to have recognized intuitively that new writers must have control over some means of book and magazine production if they are going to make themselves heard in a society in which most publishing machinery is controlled by commercial interests or by literary pressure groups that frequently reflect foreign cultures. Throughout all but the last years of *First Statement* Sutherland insisted on owning and operating his own printing equipment. The first twenty issues were mimeographed and circulated without a cover; frequency of publication changed from twice-monthly, to monthly, to semi-monthly. Subscriptions were nominally priced at one dollar per year, and many copies were given away. When a secondhand letterpress was acquired for $600, it was paid for by subscription among the editors and their friends; the prices of books issued by First Statement Press were set so low as to be no impediment to sales.

In effect, Sutherland's work with *First Statement* provided Souster and Dudek with a vivid lesson in how a little magazine can, despite limited finances, champion unfashionable writers and literary ideas against established taste. However, the responses of the two men to this lesson again demonstrate their considerable differences of temperament. Both were committed philosophically to the principles of literary freedom and change which Sutherland's *First Statement* embodied, but Dudek's immediate reaction was cautious. He was prepared neither to sacrifice steady employment and health to literary adventure as Sutherland had done,[20] nor to embrace a literary form such as a little magazine without first discovering as much as a man could about its history and theory. In August of 1943 Dudek moved to New York and enrolled at Columbia University for graduate study in journalism and history; his Master's thesis was entitled "Thackeray and the Profession of Letters." The

thesis was, in effect, a study of a man who, much like Sutherland, had attempted to combine a serious writing career with
the editing and publishing of periodicals. The next year, under
the direction of Lionel Trilling, Jacques Barzun and Emery
Neff, of the Columbia Department of English, Dudek began
the doctoral study—on the sociology of literature—that would
eventually result in the book *Literature and the Press*. This work
argued that, since the invention of the printing press, scientific
and historical forces have relentlessly debased orthodox literary
judgement to the point where serious literature can be supported only by the fugitive publications of private presses and
little magazines.

Souster's response to *First Statement* was enthusiastic and
impulsive. His first little magazine, *Direction,* was conceived
one evening late in 1943 during a boisterous discussion in his
barracks at the RCAF station in Sydney.[21] From the beginning
Direction took the form of a somewhat cruder incarnation of *First
Statement* ideas and format. Coedited by Souster with Bill
Goldberg (Irving Layton's nephew, who had been coinciden-
tally posted to Souster's base in 1943), it was mimeographed on
"borrowed" RCAF paper and equipment and mailed free of
charge to Canadian magazines, writers, editors and critics. In
addition to Souster's own poetry, it contained beginning work
by other young airmen at Souster's base plus a few poems by
Ralph Gustafson, Irving Layton and Miriam Waddington.
No. 7 contained excerpts from Henry Miller's then banned
Tropic of Cancer.

Direction's chief critical voice was Souster; although
Souster's criticism lacked the perceptive textual analyses which
made Sutherland's so persuasive, it contained similar but less
articulate judgements of A.J.M. Smith's *Book of Canadian Poetry*
(a "tired cumbersome anthology") and of those who would demand "discipline" and "restraint" of poetry. However, *Direction*
never did locate the "great deal of talent" its editors believed to
be within the air force. It depended for its best work on non-air
force writers and on Souster, who used it largely as a personal
vehicle. At the end of the war, Souster returned to Toronto and
to his position at the Imperial Bank, apparently hoping to con-

tinue *Direction* and expand it into a small press.[22] However, the other editors lost interest. Souster had lost his source of free paper and mimeograph facilities when he left the RCAF, and he failed to sell enough subscriptions to finance the printing. The tenth and final issue appeared in February 1946.

Neither during the war nor during the immediate years afterwards was there any close contact between Souster and Dudek. Both were aware of each other's contributions to *First Statement* and to its successor, *Northern Review*, to Ronald Hambleton's anthology *Unit of Five* (1944) and to Sutherland's anthology *Other Canadians* (1947). However, Dudek never became a contributor to *Direction*. Moreover, despite a three-day visit by Souster (with Bill Goldberg) to Dudek in New York City late in 1945, only an occasional card or letter seems to have passed between them. During 1943–51 Dudek was engaged mainly in research for his "literature and the press" dissertation and in course work towards his degrees. This work brought him under the influence of Lionel Trilling, whose teaching undermined Dudek's earlier commitment to Marxist idealism. Trilling convinced Dudek "that human values are not working-class values," that civilization is paradoxically the creation of tyrannies, despotisms and imperialisms, that good and evil are inevitably intertwined.[23] Dudek became fascinated by the example of Thomas Carlyle whom he began to regard as a hero — a hero who had fought against the tendency of democratic cultures to make literature into a mere commodity; moreover, he began to envision his own life as potentially a similar fight against "barbarism" conducted by writing poetry and publishing little magazines.

During these years, Souster engaged himself in activity rather than reflection. He had almost no literary acquaintances in Toronto, few literary contacts in Montreal, no links with a university and few opportunities to publish. Out of this isolation in 1948 he launched the little magazine *Enterprise* and again attempted to follow Sutherland's principle of matching the format and ambitions of a magazine to the resources and capabilities of its backers. Ostensibly motivated by a concern that Canadian poetry had "again gone on the skids" since the war's end, Souster produced each issue of *Enterprise* in editions of twenty carbon copies from his typewriter and mailed them to editors, booksellers and writers. The "magazine" received no critical attention and few contributions from other writers. The only contents of its six issues were poems, fiction and editorials by Souster, reprinted work by Henry Miller and the U.S. socialists Michael Frankel and Walter Loewenfels, and advertisements for the Enterprise Agency, Souster's similarly short-lived attempt at the part-time wholesaling of British books and magazines. Through *Enterprise* Souster made his first attempt at book publishing. The Enterprise "typescript chapbook" series was announced in *Enterprise* 2 (February 1948), but only one of its announced typewritten booklets, *New Poems* by Raymond Souster, was ever released.[24] The magazine was clearly a failure. It failed to relieve Souster's literary isolation and it also failed in its secondary role as a newsletter for the Enterprise Agency. However, the *Enterprise* experiment was useful as a dry run for Souster's later magazine projects, at least teaching him that a little magazine requires more participants than one isolated editor.

In 1949, the year after the birth and death of *Enterprise*, Louis Dudek sent a letter of admiration to Ezra Pound, who was then confined in Washington's St. Elizabeth's Hospital as a result of his postwar trial for treason. Dudek had been attracted by the economical language and realistic imagery in Pound's *Personae* before going to New York; during his doctoral studies he had read *The Cantos* and Pound's various theoretical, economic and cultural treatises, and had begun to view Pound as a modern-day Carlyle, as a "fighting artist trying to survive in a materialistic pragmatic society."[25] Dudek's letter not only precipitated a whirlwind correspondence with Pound but also resulted in his visiting St. Elizabeth's and becoming for several years Pound's "leg-man," obtaining for him many of the books, newspapers, magazines and other materials that he needed for his research and writing.[26] Then, after another year of research into the careers of nineteenth-century men of letters, during which time he also enjoyed extensive personal contact with the leading man of letters of the first half of the twentieth century,

Dudek took his first significant step into literary activism. His project — "Poetry Grapevine"[27] — was a "mailbag" to which each member of a predetermined postal circuit contributed both his own poems and criticism of the poetry others already had in the "bag." Dudek's first publishing project was a characteristically cautious undertaking which committed him to no firm editorial views or decisions other than the selection of participants. In its three rounds the mailbag reached, among others, Pound, Charles Olson, William Carlos Williams, Harold Norse and Paul Blackburn. Late in 1950 at the beginning of the second round (from which Pound and Olson had withdrawn because of other commitments), Dudek invited Souster to participate. This invitation was apparently the first communication between them in several years.

Souster's enthusiastic response ("It's like getting a letter of acceptance while in a concentration camp") reflected the extreme sense of literary isolation which he had felt during *Enterprise* and after its failure.

You have probably always enjoyed — first in Montreal and now in New York — the opportunity to meet other writers and the stimulus of exchange of ideas and opinions. I have never had this, and to some extent it is a disadvantage. There are too many writers in Canada who feel all too strongly this loneliness, this feeling of writing for an unknown audience in an alien atmosphere.[28]

Souster participated in both the second and third rounds of Dudek's New York mailbag and in the Canadian mailbag which Dudek began shortly after returning to Montreal and a post at McGill University in 1951. The mailbag project also initiated a monthly exchange of letters between Souster and Dudek which continued, with occasional interruptions, until the late 1960s. Souster appears to have regarded Dudek both as a potential friend in Canadian poetry and as a welcome source of information about contemporary U.S. and European writing. Dudek seems to have seen Souster as a potential convert to "Poundism" and as a useful contact for his re-entry into Canadian letters.

Ironically, despite vigorous attempts by Dudek during the

next few years to convince Souster of the value of Pound's writings, it was by two impulsive acts that he would most influence Souster's future course. Just after Dudek's return to Montreal in August 1951, Souster and his wife visited Quebec and met with Layton and Dudek at Dudek's grandmother's farm at Charlemagne. As Souster relates,

I'll always remember the day on the farm on the Little Jesus River, with Louis Dudek throwing the first two issues of Cid Corman's *Origin* down on the picnic table and saying "This is typical of what the nuts in New York are doing these days." I remember casually flipping through both copies and then giving them back to him—I was not yet ready for Charles Olson and Robert Creeley. But the next year something led me back to those two issues, and then Louis came to Toronto in May and left me as a gift *The Collected Later Poems of William Carlos Williams*. From that time on my world of poetry assumed largely its present shape.[29]

The contrast between the two men that is implicit in these events of 1950–51 is fundamental to their later interactions and to their uses of the little magazine. Souster felt alone ("there simply are no writers of my age and my convictions in Canada"[30]), deprived of adequate opportunities for publication and isolated from the latest developments in contemporary writing. Although Dudek also experienced extreme difficulty in getting work published, he nevertheless felt himself a part of a large international literary world. As a result of his doctoral research, he was also an authority on both the history of poetry and the role of the little magazine editor. Souster hoped through publishing to gain both self-confidence and an up-to-date literary education, whereas Dudek hoped to be able to use his own contacts, knowledge and authority to change the direction of poetry in Canada. However, Dudek lacked potential allies among Canadian writers. Of his original acquaintances from *First Statement* days, only Souster was sympathetic towards Dudek's new ideas about writing. Irving Layton, who had been one of Dudek's closest friends during the early 1940s and who had introduced him to John Sutherland, had broken with Dudek in 1947 over Dudek's acceptance of Lionel

Trilling's anti-Marxist teachings. Sutherland's interests had, since 1948, slowly turned away from experimental modernism and towards conservative values and traditional forms.

Of the two men, Souster was the more eager to begin projects which might influence the Canadian scene. His needs, particularly his need for relief from a sense of isolation, were probably greater than Dudek's, and the strength of these needs caused him to prefer direct and "daring" solutions. In June of 1951, shortly after learning that Dudek would probably be returning to Montreal, Souster suggested to him that someone should found a new magazine that would provide a strong contrast to Sutherland's *Northern Review*. Sutherland's tastes, although still progressive in the context of Canadian publishing, were now to Souster an editorial "hodge-podge."

We need an outlet for experiment and a franker discussion of the directions poetry is to take, not articles on Lampman and the movies. What we need in short is a poetry mag with daring and a little less precious an attitude.[31]

Initially, Dudek seems to have wanted only to increase the number of his literary friends in Canada and to slowly influence the literary scene from within. He did not want to become involved in confrontation. Rather than follow Souster's urgings to start a new magazine, he preferred to try to persuade Sutherland's *Northern Review* to "swing a little more into the old line."[32] Once back in Montreal he attended literary gatherings at the home of F.R. Scott and began friendships with Scott, Phyllis Webb, Hugh McLennan, A.M. Klein and Neufville Shaw.[33] In December of 1951 he launched a Canadian version of his "poetry grapevine" — now called a "postal round table" — and included among its members James Reaney, Anne Wilkinson, James Wreford, P.K. Page, Roy Daniells, Irving Layton, Alan Crawley, E.J. Pratt, Neufville Shaw, A.J.M. Smith, A.G. Bailey, Miriam Waddington, Dorothy Livesay, Kay Smith, Ralph Gustafson, Robert Finch, A.M. Klein, Phyllis Webb, Margaret Avison, Anne Marriott, Sutherland, Scott, Souster, Earle Birney and W.W.E. Ross.[34] In early January 1952 Dudek capped this get-reacquainted-with-Canadian-letters program by an enthusiastic renewal of friendship with Irving Layton, which was brought about largely through the efforts of Layton's wife, Betty Sutherland.

In October 1951 Souster announced to Dudek his intention to establish the little magazine *Contact* as an alternative to *Northern Review*. Its "unofficial motto" was to be Pound's "MAKE IT NEW" — a strong signal on Souster's part that he intended to counter Sutherland's conservative and static policies with an experimental literature of innovation and renewal.[35] Dudek responded by remarking, "I don't think it'll affect Sutherland in any way unless for the better...." He did not offer to collaborate but did immediately begin working behind the scenes to influence the magazine by offering advice and manuscripts both by himself and by others. However, Sutherland was apparently proving impervious to his overtures of friendship and literary aid, and Dudek's attitude to him quickly hardened. A month later he wrote to Souster, "J. Sutherland is dead as a doorknob. He's waiting for something to drop into his lap."[36] When the first issue of *Contact* reached him on 16 January 1952, Dudek declared Sutherland a "sluggard" and *Contact* "a smash the windows and let's breathe" achievement.[37]

Dudek provided reviews and editorials for the early issues of *Contact* and suggested numerous writers from whom Souster should solicit manuscripts. Souster rejected Dudek's most extreme suggestions, such as his idea of one issue devoted entirely to an "Ezra Pound Comes North" symposium.[38] As editor, Souster endeavoured to tread a narrow line between international credibility and support of new native talent. He eagerly used Dudek's various U.S. contacts in order to educate himself about contemporary writing, but resisted having these writers, particularly the "Poundists" among whom Dudek then included himself, dominate any one issue of the magazine with what Souster termed "cult" ideas. Through Dudek's help he obtained work from Judson Crews, Paul Blackburn and Cid Corman. Corman, who was editor of the U.S. little magazine *Origin* and one of the first editors to publish the Black Mountain writers Charles Olson and Robert Creeley, took an immediate interest in Souster and in *Contact* and soon brought to Souster's attention a very large number of U.S., French, Italian and

German writers. Souster also very sensibly continued to imitate Sutherland's *First Statement* policy of using the least complex and least expensive production methods possible. He acquired a mimeograph machine before launching the magazine, and produced each issue in his basement. Despite strong advice from Dudek, and later from Robert Creeley, that he contract for letterpress production, he yielded only to the extent that he allowed Dudek, after *Contact* no. 1, to obtain a printed cover designed by Betty Sutherland.

The very large international element in *Contact* — more than fifty per cent of the contributors — underlines one of Dudek's and Souster's chief criticisms of *Northern Review:* its almost exclusive concern with Canadian writing. In an attempt to analyze his boredom with the "conventional smoothness" of most *Northern Review* poetry, Dudek wrote to Souster:

My theory is that looking for "native quality" just shuts the eyes to what is new and different and alive. Who the hell cares whether its native or not? And do we want to be natives forever? . . .

Note this NR p. 25: "the slavish trend of consciously or unconsciously imitating the English writer . . . " and p. 26: Katharine Mansfield, alas, "belonged to the European tradition." What other is there? We've got to *belong to the European tradition!!!!* then see lower on p. 26, the writer is encouraged that "Some of the earthiness of native tradition was now manifesting itself." Gord. Earthiness, mud. What is maniinfesting [*sic*] all colonial and provincial literatures.[39]

Souster wrote back, "This is certainly the big problem with Canadian poets today, they do not know one another and they are unable to learn from others."[40]

Ironically, the issue of colonialism versus native talent was the subject of many of *First Statement*'s polemics against the *Preview* group. It had been as native writers of "hard-fisted proletarianism," as poets who didn't mind "calling a spade a spade" that Sutherland had presented Layton and Souster in *Other Canadians.*[41] As his early articles in *First Statement* reveal, Dudek was first attracted to Sutherland by his opposition to poetry derived from "Europe" and "the accumulated lore of Western civilization."[42] Over the years not only had Sutherland changed from an anti-British/pro-American to an anti-British/anti-American position, but Dudek and Souster had changed from a purely American orientation to a simultaneously American and continental European one. In a sense, the narrowness of Sutherland's "native" preferences was not as inconsistent with his original stance as Dudek and Souster believed; their perceptions of Sutherland were distorted by the new broadening of their own perspectives.

Contact was, then, like *First Statement, Direction* and *Enterprise,* a definite expression of literary discontent. Both Souster and Dudek saw the few existing Canadian periodicals as inadequate both to their personal publication needs and to the hopes they had for the future direction of Canadian writing. While they reacted to this situation differently — Dudek by working behind the scenes, Souster by direct action — the message which they projected through *Contact* was clear: Canadian poetry magazines were conventional and parochial; Canadian writers were isolated and technically naive; international writing was rapidly leaving a static Canadian literature behind.

Within a few months of the first issue of *Contact,* Cid Corman's influence on the magazine began to create a minor rift between Souster and Dudek. The fundamental cause of the conflict was Souster's immense curiosity about international writing, the same curiosity which made him such an ardent correspondent with Dudek throughout 1951. What Dudek offered Souster was essentially an enthusiasm for Ezra Pound and a few related writers. Early in 1952 when Souster's correspondence with Corman developed into an often weekly exchange, Souster was introduced to a larger and more exciting literary world inhabited by Charles Olson, Robert Creeley, William Bronk, Denise Levertov, Samuel French Morse, Wallace Stevens, Vincent Ferrini, Gottfried Benn, George Forestier, Octavio Paz, René de Obaldia and Guillaume Apollinaire. This world proved much more satisfying to Souster than did Dudek's smaller literary circle. Souster seems to have been stimulated by Corman's frequently critical remarks about the Canadian work in *Contact,* such as his comment after no. 2: "most of the poems seem amateur to me."[43]

Souster appears also to have been impressed by Corman's injunction to use "only the most probing and exacting integrity and sense of values"[44] in his editorial decisions, and by his instructions not to patronize existing Canadian writing but "to get the writers where you are into the Canadian bloodstream; they are still writing 25–30 years behind the times."[45]

In brief, it seems that Souster's insecurity about his writing and his literary education was relieved much more by Corman's ruthless but usually constructive criticism than it was by Dudek's assurances that *Contact* was "tops . . . the best mag in Canada"[46] or his warning that Olson "was off on a wrong steer."[47] Corman quickly became Souster's most important and prolific correspondent: to date they have exchanged almost one thousand letters. Nevertheless, Souster vigorously resisted Corman's attempts to internationalize *Contact* totally, just as he had resisted similar attempts by Dudek. He persisted in publishing the Canadian work that Corman scorned and firmly rejected a rather impractical suggestion that *Contact* amalgamate with *Origin* and the English little magazine *Window* under Souster's general editorship.[48]

Dudek's role during this period was that of the unwavering advocate of *Contact*'s Canadian responsibility. Even in the case of his proposed Pound issue, the contributors were to be predominantly Canadian. He was suspicious of many of the U.S. writers which Corman recommended to Souster ("We've always had reservations about *Origin* [Creeley and Olson were too odd and eccentric for the straight and simple Canadian in us]"[49]). The international work was intended chiefly to teach and stimulate Canadian writers and to counter the conservatism of *Northern Review*. Dudek argued strongly against Corman's amalgamation proposal and afterwards, in November 1952, put forward a counterproposal that he and Layton become associate editors with full authority over their own contributions. *Contact* was not to be a "showcase of museum pieces, 'fine poetry' [apparently a reference to the U.S. writers] but a workshop, as active poetry and ideas."[50] Again Souster refused to share his editorial responsibility. On 2 December 1952 Dudek wrote, "the mag is not for the open public, it's a workshop for young, for solitary minds. Don't worry too much about standards." [51]

Dudek appears to have given up this tug of war over *Contact* early in 1953 when four young Montreal writers — Aileen Collins, Wanda Staniszewska, Stan Rozynski and Jackie Gallagher — approached him for assistance in starting a little magazine. Dudek agreed, and later christened the magazine *CIV/n,* an abbreviation of "civilization" taken from a line in an Ezra Pound letter: "*CIV/n* not a one-man job." As Dudek's account of the magazine's structure suggests, *CIV/n* was not a one-man job but a "workshop" or "cooperative" most dissimilar to Souster's or Corman's solitary editorships.

I offered help and advice, and proposed that manuscripts be read by a larger group including Layton and myself, and that Aileen Collins and the Rozynskis edit the magazine in the light of our group discussions. There was always a tactful solicitude on the part of Layton and myself not to interfere with the editorial freedom of the actual editors. We read the poetry before a group at Layton's house enjoying free comments and debate over the poems, but we made no decisions and left the final choice of what was to go into the magazine up to the Editor. [52]

CIV/n provided Dudek with another opportunity to influence Canadian writing indirectly. It not only embodied the desired "workshop" atmosphere but also seems to have allowed him to advance his own views without significant opposition. *CIV/n* also embodied the Canadian emphasis he had wished *Contact* to adopt. Almost all the contributors to *CIV/n* were Canadian; when the international writing world was represented, it was usually as the subject of a review or commentary.

Ironically enough, this emphasis on local writing displeased Pound almost as much as the Canadian writing in *Contact* displeased Corman. Pound wrote,

CIV/V [*sic*] o.k. for local centre / question whether D/ has contact with anyone or any means interested in a mag/ standing for maximum awareness, and suggested that *CIV/n* affiliate itself as a "feeder" with various financially troubled magazines (*Shenandoah, European*) in the publishing of one international journal to be edited by *Shenandoah's* T.H. Carter and to which "CIV/n might claim right to one page per issue." [53] This proposition, somewhat similar to Corman's *Window* proposal to Souster, seems to have provoked no interest in Dudek.

After founding *CIV/n*, Dudek continued to write to Souster and to contribute to *Contact*, but he ceased to propose structural changes or editorial initiatives. Souster continued *Contact* for another year, achieving a total of ten issues, but without the previous controversial and contentious dialogues with Corman and Dudek. Both the character of the magazine and the number of its subscribers (around fifty) remained static. Its hoped for "break-through in strength" [54] to British and U.S. critical recognition did not occur. Souster's letters to Dudek reveal that his energies were now being taken up by another project, one which had grown from *Contact* and which quickly had become more important than the magazine, namely Contact Press.

The idea for a press jointly operated by Souster, Dudek and Layton which would publish their own books and those of newly emerging Canadian writers whom they admired has usually been credited to Dudek, although the exact origins of the idea are obscure. The first extant mention of a Contact Press project occurs in a January 1952 letter from Souster to Layton approving Dudek's idea of a joint book of poems by Souster, Layton and himself but questioning the need to publish it at their own expense. Souster writes to Layton again on 4 February 1952 requesting more action on "this 'Trio' project," [55] and on 9 February 1952, in a postscript to a long letter to Souster, Dudek writes,

"Trio" might work out, TRIO? Or some name of a 3 headed beast, 25 poems each. Shall we pick poems out of that mss. from New Dir? [56]

Dudek's previous letter to Souster on 3 February had related his failure to place a large manuscript of Souster's work with

New Directions (the "New Dir" reference above) but oddly did
not mention a "Trio" proposal.

   Souster thought that "Trio" — or "Cerberus," as Dudek
soon christened it — should be published either by McClelland
& Stewart in their Indian File series[57] or by Ryerson Press (at
that time the only commercial press to have published Souster
and Dudek). Dudek, even in the 9 February postscript, was
adamant that the book should be published at their own expense, and on 11 February sent Souster a diatribe against commercial publishing in which the "Cerberus" proposal was the
main issue.

Did I send you my chapbook, stinking thin business for $1?? Yes,
goddamit, let's get ourselves out a book of our own, the three of us,
and piss on the presses. The poet has to publish his own work hence-
forth if he wants to print what he wrote, and if he wants to print more
than 12 pages in SIX YEARS. I'm not Pope's man who
   "Just writes to make his barrenness appear
   And strains, from hard-boiled brains, eight lines a year"
tho' Ryerson makes us both look like it. I don't blame Ryerson's in
fact; no need for them to subsidize literature. The whole system
stinks, when 100000000 advertisements get mass distribution and a
few poems get 250 copies on toilet paper.[58]

   Dudek's anger here reflects extreme but justifiable frustration. He and Souster, despite their own mailbag and magazine
ventures, and despite their having been published in Canada
since 1943, had received only token attention from commercial
publishers. Their magazines had enabled them to communicate with other writers and to articulate publicly their critical
and aesthetic positions, but not to publish the major portion of
their poetic work, which remained stacked in filing cabinets
and desk drawers. This frustration reached as far back as 1943,
when both had sent large manuscripts to Ryerson only to have
a small part of these culled out by Ronald Hambleton for publication in the anthology *Unit of Five*. Souster's luck appeared to
change in 1947 when Ryerson accepted his fifty-nine-page
manuscript *Go to Sleep World;* however, this book included
mainly poems he had written in his air force days and was

totally inadequate, from his point of view, in reducing the "backlog" of poems he was accumulating.[59] Both Souster and Dudek had chapbooks accepted and published by Ryerson in 1951–52, but these booklets represented ruthless editings of the full-size collections which they had submitted and included only a small part of the work they had available for publication. In Souster's case many of the poems were seven to eight years old. Dudek had attempted to get one of Souster's manuscripts published in the U.S. He submitted the manuscript to several U.S. publishers, but each praised and then rejected it. James Laughlin of New Directions wrote, "Souster is an excellent poet," to which Dudek grumbled in reporting the rejection to Souster, "How many 'excellent' poets does he know?"[60]

The postwar years had not been adventurous ones in the commercial publication of poetry in Canada. Poets influenced by traditional British prosody were published in book-length collections: Robert Finch, Patrick Anderson, P.K. Page, James Wreford, E.J. Pratt, A.M. Klein and Earle Birney (the latter three times). The Ryerson chapbook series, essentially inadequate except for the publication of first books or single long poems, appeared much more significant in Canada than it would have in a healthy publishing scene. Ryerson's eclectic policies, which gathered in dilettantes, traditionalists and committed experimentalists, did little to enhance the reputations of its poets. Writers like Dudek and Souster, and their friend Irving Layton, who wished to bring new modes and aesthetics to the poetry-reading public, were virtually shut out of a publishing world whose smallness was exceeded only by its conventionality.

Dudek's enthusiasm for printing *Cerberus* privately soon convinced Souster; on 15 March he wrote to Layton:

You and Dudek go ahead with Cerberus — let me know my share of the cost. . . . Why not say the book is published by "Contact Press" (if you want to tie it in with *Contact*) etc.[61]

Dudek accepted the Contact imprimatur and also proposed that *Cerberus* should be the start of "a list of books under this imprint."[62] Within a few months he had suggested several titles, including the anthology *Canadian Poems 1850–1952* edited by himself and Layton, Layton's *Love the Conqueror Worm,* his own *Twenty-four Poems* and Souster's *Shake Hands with the Hangman* (published in mimeograph in 1953), plus collections "of Page, of Anderson, of [Malcolm] Miller, of Webb etc. etc."[63] This was definitely to be a polemical publishing program. Once again, as in the case of *First Statement,* First Statement Press and *Contact* magazine, writers were going to attempt to control the means through which poetry was printed in order both to provide new alternatives to the commercial tastes of the established media and to revise the relative reputations of poets. Dudek was very clear to Souster about the former intention:

The little mag is a development where the writers undertake their own publication in periodicals. The book follows. This is a measure of the commercial corruption of the estab. presses.[64]

Such a position was consistent with his findings in his doctoral thesis *Literature and the Press* which in 1952 he was still writing.

The little magazines are ... the most recent and most energetic sign of the reaction of literary minorities against the levelling standards of the new urban culture, a culture thrown out of balance by new machines and new wealth. . . .[65]

Souster incorporated these principles directly into the pamphlet he wrote to introduce Contact Press and its first book to the public. The effect of this pamphlet — an effect which most successful poetry "movements" and their presses in the twentieth century have attempted to create — was immediately to mythologize both the press and its poet-editors:

Readers of this leaflet both Canadians and Americans, are no doubt aware of the wholesale commercialization of the press today with its consequent cheapening of the values of the mind. Canadian poetry ... has in our time reflected this situation clearly. . . .
    It is thus left for the poets themselves to take matters into their own hands and fight against this increasingly dangerous situation.[66]

The mythologizing tended to beg the literary quality of the poetry and to present the writing solely as political act. But political acts are not necessarily literary acts. As we shall see in later chapters, in Dudek and Souster's own poetry the transformation of political belief into literary act became very often the central problem of their writing—a problem which Dudek struggled with in his long poems and which Souster in many of his later poems failed to resolve.

Dudek's attempts to revise the relative reputations of Canadian poets were more subtle than Souster's. The *Canadian Poems 1850-1952* anthology was Dudek's most obvious instrument, and it played the role which such ostensibly "catholic" anthologies often do in establishing the credibility of a new group or school. Here Dudek, Souster and Layton could be listed beside Lampman, Carman, Pratt and Birney as additions to the canon of Canadian poetry. Moreover, Souster (with six poems) could be given more weight than James Wreford, P.K. Page, Robert Finch or Birney (all of whom had already won Governor General's Awards) and also more weight than A.J.M. Smith (three poems), Bliss Carman (four), Charles G.D. Roberts (five), Ralph Gustafson (three) or F.R. Scott (three). Souster, in fact, became the third best-represented poet in the anthology, after Pratt and Lampman. Layton and Dudek modestly allowed themselves four poems each, thus taking a rank ahead of almost all the new poets of the 1940s (Finch, Gustafson, Waddington, Reaney, Le Pan and Webb) and equal to that of Page, Smith and Carman.

But the conscious and unconscious ambitions of Dudek and Souster, together with Layton, were greater than merely finding a place in the canon of Canadian poets. They wanted to become historically important both as emancipators of Canadian poetry and as the most original and talented writers of their time. As a group they needed not only to establish a mythology in which they appeared as leaders of art and poetry against the forces of materialism and corruption but also to establish themselves as major poets. This kind of change in Canadian critical perspective would necessarily take longer to achieve than had the canonical revisions attempted in *Canadian*

Poems 1850–1952. Nevertheless, the creation of Contact Press soon allowed Dudek, Layton and Souster to publish more frequently than "competing" poets of greater or similar reputation. It allowed them, because they controlled design and typography, a clearer and more effective presentation of their work than the poets of the commercial presses enjoyed. It also enabled them to present each other as "mature" poets much earlier in their careers than might otherwise have been possible; such a presentation first occurred with Contact's publication of Souster's *Selected Poems* in 1956 and would have been repeated in a similar Layton volume in 1959 had he not withdrawn from the press. This kind of polemic intent was spelled out by Dudek during the planning of the Souster *Selected Poems*:

The impression this should make of what you can do, should be magnificent, and will place you high up there, with us and outside Canada. It will have to come to be realized, I don't know when, that what counts in poetry in this country from 1940–1960 or so is yourself, Layton, and I. Smith & Scott are very thin predecessors. "Meticulous moderns" as I call them in college classes. Page & Anderson really don't count; they *did nothing* with what they had, and spoiled their best with mannerism, cerebration, pretentiousness, piling on of metaphors, etc. Klein had failed. All of them are very nice, mind you, and good to have around; but the real trail is the one we blazed. . . .[67]

Because of the limited number of poetry-selling bookstores in Canada, distribution was simplified. As often happens with small poetry presses, the fact that poetry books were its major product, rather than a minor appendage to a bourgeois commercial publishing program, meant that Contact could locate its market more precisely than could its commercial competitors. Contact Press books nearly always outsold such competing publications as the Ryerson Press chapbooks.

With the founding of Contact Press and the discontinuation of both *Contact* and *CIV/n* early in 1954, the relationship between Dudek and Souster stabilized. They were loosely affiliated with Layton in a missionary publishing venture and while able to agree on certain literary generalities, they were not close in matters of specific reading projects or detailed literary theory. Ezra Pound continued to be Dudek's most influential literary correspondent; Cid Corman continued to be Souster's. The frequency of letters between Dudek and Souster slackened to one a month or less, and these chiefly concerned Contact Press business.

Most of the Contact Press books published before 1959 were the result of personal initiatives by either Dudek or Souster, conceived and sometimes executed without consultation. Both men simply used the Contact Press imprint to sanction their private publishing projects. Dudek independently published D.G. Jones's *Frost on the Sun*, F.R. Scott's *Eye of the Needle*, R.G. Everson's *Lattice for Momos*, plus his own *Europe, Transparent Sea, En México* and *Laughing Stalks*. Souster published the anthology *Poets 56*, W.W.E. Ross's *Experiment 1923–29*, Peter Miller's *Meditations at Noon*, plus his own *Dream That Is Dying, For What Time Slays, Walking Death* and *Crepe-Hanger's Carnival*. They appear to have collaborated only on Souster's *Selected Poems* and on *Trio*, the three-section anthology of work by Gael Turnbull, Eli Mandel and Phyllis Webb. Irving Layton contributed only his own books, except for Henry Moscovitch's *Serpent Ink*.

Because Souster and Dudek disapproved of the Moscovitch book, the editorial process at Contact Press was revised in 1958. The editors agreed on the new system verbally before Dudek formalized it in a letter to Souster. Despite the introduction of a veto provision, the editors still maintained a permissive policy, and one disarmingly supportive of their own work.

(1) As a rule we publish if two of us are for the book; (2) if one of us thinks very strongly that the book is good, he may publish against two votes negative; (3) also, if one person feels that a book is deplorably bad, he may *veto* an acceptance by the other two; (4) clearly we are stalemated if a *veto* comes up against a *volo* — but I doubt whether that will ever happen; if so (5) the positive vote, to print, goes. Also, the occasional book that one feels is very good and unquestionable need not go the rounds of the three of us; in fact we probably don't need to read mss. that we know beforehand will be OK; eg. a book by F.R. Scott . . . or one of our own. [68]

For a variety of reasons Layton withdrew from Contact

Press late in 1958. For one thing, he no longer needed Contact as a publisher of his own work. Robert Creeley had published Layton's *In the Midst of My Fever* at Divers Press in 1954; Jonathan Williams had published two large collections, *The Improved Binoculars* (1956) and *A Laughter in the Mind* (1958), at Jargon Press in Highlands, North Carolina, and was about to publish *A Red Carpet for the Sun* jointly with McClelland & Stewart. Also, Layton's increasing friendship with such U.S. writers as Creeley, Corman, Jonathan Williams and William Carlos Williams (who had written a laudatory introduction to *The Improved Binoculars*) tended to alienate Dudek. To Dudek, who not only deeply mistrusted Corman and resented his influence on *Contact* but also generally disliked the work of *Origin* poets such as Creeley and Olson, these friendships seemed clandestine and disloyal. A third factor was Layton's separation in 1958 from Betty Sutherland, which divided Dudek's loyalties, and a fourth was Layton's success — particularly through his polemical introductions to his books — in mythologizing himself. While both Dudek and Souster had recognized the necessity of a Contact mythology, they felt uncomfortable with the extravagance of Layton's methods and were unwilling to identify themselves with them. Layton himself had often been unwilling to associate himself with a group mythology or image. In 1952 he had reportedly objected to the phrase "the new movement" in a proposed advertisement for *Cerberus* and told Dudek that he did not believe in movements. [69]

Layton's place in Contact was given, in August 1959, to Peter Miller, a poet already published by Contact who worked in the same Toronto branch of the Imperial Bank as Souster. With Miller's arrival, considerable reorganization occurred. Miller not only volunteered to help select manuscripts but also to finance most of the books personally, to oversee all book production, and to manage all financial records and distribution. This effectively centralized Contact's operations and allowed Souster and Miller to dominate an editorship which had previously been largely dominated by Dudek and Layton. The Dudek principle that whoever controls book production also controls manuscript selection was immediately confirmed. A continuing debate began about editorial privileges, in which

Dudek usually argued that books written by the three editors did "not need to be circulated . . . or approved" [70] and that books strongly favoured by any one editor should not be subject to a majority veto. Miller argued for editorial unanimity. [71] The matter was uneasily settled when Dudek agreed to accept majority decision. [72] This became the usual practice except in the case of Dudek's vigorous opposition to a Margaret Atwood manuscript in 1964. In that instance, a minority opinion prevailed. [73]

Throughout these latter years of the press, Dudek was continually anxious that the press was becoming too demanding, if not conventional, in its editorial standards. He feared that Contact might lose claim to its antiestablishment and avant-garde mythology. On 21 November 1960, he wrote to Souster concerning one rejected manuscript, "If we refuse . . . pretty soon we'll find that we're not bringing any of the new poets out, and that they're starting presses on their own." For similar reasons, he was leery of making any overtures for financial assistance to the newly established Canada Council.

As soon as you submit to gov't subsidy you've got civil service mentality to deal with: the MS has to be immaculate, with starched shirt and full-dress suit, *and before long the poetry too will toe the mark.* They are bound to help poetry that has nothing to say and that is perfectly finished as a new-laid corpse. [74]

The Governor General's Award, which Dudek had throughout the 1950s called the "glove in 'er genitals Award," was another sore point between Dudek and Miller. Dudek wanted to preserve Contact's antiestablishment mythology, but Miller felt that Contact's never having won the award was an injustice:

_____ 's books give me the shits. So does the Governor General and his obscene Board and his pornographic Award. Obviously Contact will never get a gee-gee, on general principles. . . . [75]

Ironically, Contact would receive the award in its last year of operation for a book which Dudek opposed as alien to Contact's "principles": Margaret Atwood's *Circle Game.*

Dudek's concern that Contact should not become too ex-clusive and yet at the same time should avoid work that was "fake," "spurious," "the reverse of what I think Contact stands for,"[76] brought him into conflict with Miller over financing. Dudek wished to follow Contact's original policy of allowing Contact authors to pay in full or in part the cost of publishing their books because this policy allowed a large number of Contact books to be published. He discounted the possibility that an editorial decision might be influenced by a poet's wealth.

I'm all for loosening up this professional joint of ours, in getting more books done by the alive and kicking young men around now, and looking more at the possibilities than at the museum-quality of the books. To do this you would have to let Contact Press be an open-door medium through which they could best do what they wanted — once we felt that any particular book was worth doing, or a poet worth encouraging.[77]

Miller felt that allowing poets to pay publication costs was potentially damaging to the reputation of the press because it raised the suspicion of vanity publishing. This conflict between a policy of publishing "alive and kicking young men" and a policy of preserving the press's integrity and "reputation" struck at the heart of the small press concept. Dudek's was the more correct avant-garde position, Miller's that of one overly con-cerned with establishment recognition and approval.

On 4 October 1964 Souster entered the controversy by writing to Dudek,

Contact's role . . . is to bring along the young until they can make it with the commercial publishers. Or to publish work by older poets whose work is too uncompromising or "advanced" for the commercial houses and would otherwise be denied a hearing.

While this was definitely congruent with Dudek's sense of the activist small press, Souster's next comments were not. He de-fined "the young" as "those who have worked at the craft for six or seven years" and suggested that two Contact books per year would be too many rather than not enough. [78] Dudek wrote back,

Contact Press is obviously going to continue on its present formal course. I believe in a little more elbow room, freedom to publish on the part of authors who show promise, open-house when good things pour in and less when they don't. Obviously this is not any longer the method of Contact Press. We have finished with the frontier!

This was essentially the same argument he had used in 1953 in criticizing the "standards" of Souster's *Contact* shortly before involving himself in the unofficial editing of the "workshop" magazine *CIV/n*. In this same letter he announced that he intended to found a new press, Delta Canada, [79] in partnership with Michael Gnarowski and Glen Siebrasse, and pointedly remarked, "I believe in *private publishing* as the only way for a rich poetic environment to develop." [80]

The years 1965 and 1966 were a time of constant quarreling between Souster and Dudek over editorial judgements. Although Dudek wished to have the press publish more books, he disagreed violently with many of the books the other editors proposed. Most of his objections were rooted in his earlier suspicion of the Americans Charles Olson and Robert Creeley. Dudek mistakenly saw both these poets as fundamentally anarchic in writing method and poetic structure and accused them of standing for a poetry "based on personal anarchism, a state of mind and a process of association cut off from all public and common ground." [81] They seemed to him to lack the rational perspective and linear sense of cultural history that Dudek personally required of major poets. He believed that both men, as students of Pound, had overdeveloped not only the primitivist dimension of imagist aesthetics but also Pound's ideogrammic method, to the exclusion of intellectual commentary and coherence. These faults were copied uncritically, he felt, by many of Souster's *New Wave Canada* poets. Of a manuscript by Victor Coleman he wrote, "the whole thing is merely an import from USA, and from Vancouver, of that goddamned new style foisted on the ignorant young by Olson, also partly by Creeley." [82] Of a book Contact published by Richard Clarke he wrote that it was "sincere, pathetic maundering," "bits of commonplace facts floating in the void." Dudek was clearly disturbed by the book and expressed amazement that Souster and Miller could like a manuscript that was such a departure from the Contact policy of poetry with "guts, vitality, and staying power."[83] Souster answered that Contact "should stay in the vanguard of what was being done in Canadian poetry . . . being open to new developments." This vanguard was not, according to Souster, in Montreal among the young who work "from Layton." "Canadian poetry in five years is going to be Coleman and Clarke and others of this new 'cool' approach; it isn't going to be Mayne and Coupey."[84]

The collapse of Contact Press in 1967 was precipitated not by editorial dispute but by Peter Miller's decision, for family reasons, to withdraw from the "role of financing and physically producing books for Contact Press."[85] Despite his failure to agree with Souster on what constituted "vanguard" poetry, Dudek at once suggested that the press continue and that Toronto poet Victor Coleman be asked if he would take over Miller's administrative duties.[86] Souster, perhaps wearied by the conflicts of the preceding years, replied on 31 October 1966 that he wanted more time for his own writing.

I think Contact Press has done the job it was founded to do — we have bridged a very difficult time in Canadian letters — and now it's largely history. What better time to call a halt.[87]

On 5 November Dudek wrote to Souster to concur with his decision. This letter, more than anything, demonstrates the wisdom of their discontinuing the press, as well as the extent to which their differences had developed. It began elegiacally: "we've all been getting older and the literary scene has been shifting, so that more and more the Press has become a very different thing from year to year." Later,

Your NEW WAVE was a kind of hell-to-pay attempt to get in line and in touch with the new generation. But this new generation is not our generation, is not wanting our kind of poetry. Maybe it's not even a continuation from the direct and straight poetry of conviction of the forties. I see it as a messy sort of doodling, available to anybody and everybody, a sociological movement rather than a poetry movement, with scores of floundering young poets everywhere smearing pages with reams of incoherent personal drivel. . . .

We can't edit what we don't respect or admire. . . . [88]

To Souster, of course, the *New Wave Canada* anthology, sub-titled "The New Explosion in Canadian Poetry," had been an activist and polemical publication parallel to Contact's first publication, *Cerberus*, and entirely in the "energetic" and "open house" tradition of small press publishing which Dudek be-lieved in.

Two magazines founded by Souster and Dudek during the Contact Press years further illustrate the differences between the two men which eventually undermined their association. Souster announced his plans for *Combustion* (1957–1960) late in 1956 in letters to Dudek, Corman and Charles Olson. A major reason for *Combustion* seems to have been Cid Corman's deci-sion to terminate *Origin* after its twentieth issue. *Combustion* seems to have been designed to take up the slack left by *Origin*'s demise, although not in any sense to be a total replacement. Dudek's letters to Souster throughout 1957–60 reflect very little interest in *Combustion*. He directs few manuscripts to it and makes no suggestions about editorial policy. Olson's re-sponse, however, was exceedingly warm: "The greatest, to hear from you. And that you are going to have another one. Wow. Makes up for the loss of CONTACT." [89] He sent several poems to the magazine and on hearing indirectly in October 1960 of Souster's plans to end it, wrote, "Damned upset to hear you have stopped COMBUSTION . . . please wire bad news, next time. Awful: why did you do it?" [90] Corman wrote to Souster weekly during the *Combustion* years, directing manu-scripts that might have otherwise been published in *Origin*, sending names of potential subscribers and contributors, appraising each issue page by page and offering his own poems and translations of European poets.

Like Souster's earlier magazines, *Combustion* was carefully kept within a small and practical budget. It was mimeographed on Souster's own basement equipment in limited editions of 100 to 125 copies and mailed without cover or wrapper to anyone sufficiently interested to request it. Like *Contact*, *Combustion* was international in content. In the first three issues Souster tried to keep a balance between Canadian and international writers. Contributors included the Canadians Layton, Dudek, Gael Turnbull, W.W.E. Ross, F.R. Scott, Ralph Gustafson, Jay Macpherson; the Americans Jonathan Williams, Corman, Olson, Allen Ginsberg, Ron Loewensohn, Jack Kerouac, Michael McClure, Gregory Corso, Theodore Enslin, Larry Eigner, Denise Levertov; plus translations of Mathias Lübeck, André Salmon, Jacques Prévert, Rocco Scotellare, Serge Essenin— rendered mostly by W.W.E. Ross and Corman. But the international poets dominated the later issues and eventually included Creeley, Robert Duncan, Gary Snyder, Fielding Dawson and Louis Zukofsky. These were largely writers of the Black Mountain/*Origin* axis, and thus when Corman announced late in 1959 plans to reactivate *Origin*, Souster seems to have seen further issues of *Combustion* as redundant. The last regular issue of *Combustion* (no. 14) appeared in August 1960; the first issue of the second series of *Origin* was issued in April 1961.

Dudek's main reaction to *Combustion* was to begin his own magazine, *Delta*. He announced the project to Souster in a letter which shows his concern about editorial control of printing equipment as well as his misgivings about *Combustion*.

. . . I Clodovicus Delta for Dudek have bought a PRINTING PRESS which is now stowed away in the cellarage, upon which I intend to move into the crowded little (Canadian) magazine market, so push over a little please. I think there's room for another one, besides your Comb. & Yes and so forth. (Incidentally, your latest Combustion interesting as usual, though I would & may— object to the surplus of translation, the overplus of Prévert everywhere, and the superplus of Char.

It's [*Delta*] a magazine in which I'll be able to bring out my new foundlings (from McGill etc.) and to develop my own viewpoint. . . . [91]

A month later he wrote,

Combustion for the most part discourages me, with its amount of words, crowdedness, messiness (in some poems), volume of French hand-me-downs (as usual), the feeling of chaotic disorder... worth putting out anyway. How would we know otherwise how bad it is? [92]

Dudek's lead editorial in *Delta* no. 1 (October 1957), "Why a New Poetry Magazine?," made both indirect and direct reference to the internationalism of *Combustion*. "*Delta* is primarily a local affair: it is a poetry magazine for Canada with a job to do here." Later: "Unlike Souster's *Combustion* (valuable and kindred as that may be), we will not stuff our pages with translation, with Jacques Prévert and René Char, etc., set in good or bad English prose."

The contrast in viewpoints here was, as in the days of *Contact* and *CIV/n,* the difference between a man who wished to learn and one who wished to teach. For Souster, *Combustion* represented an intensive course in world literature, with Corman as the chief instructor. Each new foreign poet—Char, Prévert, Montale, Paz, Ginsberg, Zukofsky—was a fresh discovery. Dudek, however, regarded most of these writers as part of his past and those new to him as awkwardly derivative of earlier and known writers. He had read what he felt was worth reading of contemporary world literature and was ready to turn this knowledge to the development of his own and other Canadian writing.

Delta became known as a "personal magazine." In the twenty-six issues published between October 1957 and October 1966, ninety per cent of the space in *Delta*, with the exception of one Ezra Pound issue (no. 22), was devoted to Canadian writing. Between poems, Dudek printed brief editorial statements about science, literature and economics, plus numerous quotations from writers who agreed with his opinion that sociological analyses offered a key to the difficulties which serious writers had consistently encountered in this century. A common theme in *Delta* was the idea that great art resulted from "the precision of reason and consciousness." On this premise Dudek opposed both the Olsonian concept of "projective verse" ("rudimentary," "disordered and groping," "cloddish and limited") and the mythopoeic writing associated with

Northrop Frye ("crude stories of the emotional dreamers," "childlike," belonging to "the illiterate, the neurotic, and the stupid"). [93] During these years, Dudek came more and more to look upon poetry as a conscious, rational art that employed preconscious process merely as raw material; his increasingly outspoken expression of this belief alienated him almost totally from Souster, who had always regarded Pound as too intellectual, and who complained to Corman in 1965,

And since when are warm nostalgic feelings out of place in poetry. Does all modern poetry have to have the abstract still-life qualities of modern art, with all its feelings carefully held and hidden. . . . I know I get sloppy very often, too sentimental, but I *hope* I never get Ezra Pound *cold*, Robert Creeley *controlled*. Denise Levertov seems to me to be pursuing the best path. . . . [94]

Perhaps this difference between a Souster impressed with the colloquial music and imagery of W.C. Williams — a Souster who wished to "get the poem outdoors" [95] — and a Dudek who admired poetry which, like Pound's, incorporated intellectual analysis, realistic detail and sociological and historical concern was the crucial one for their relationship in the long term. It was masked as long as they were both fighting for attention in a literary world dominated by conventional magazines and publishers. However, once their publishing efforts became somewhat successful, Dudek became increasingly distressed by Souster's generous and essentially nonintellectual response to poetry — a response expressed in subjective adjectives such as "vigorous," "exciting" and "experimental" and directed largely to the rhythm and imagery of a work rather than to its semantic content. In turn, Souster tried to resist the rationalist strain in Dudek which caused him to see Olson and Creeley as "odd and eccentric," [96] Corman as "a straining, youthful hysterical mess," [97] and Gwendolyn MacEwen as "extremely *incoherent* in both thought and expression." [98]

Corman himself, through his letters to Layton and Souster, tended to exacerbate these disagreements. As we shall see in chapter 6, he lamented Souster's inclinations towards easy moralizing and cliché and urged him both to give more detailed and sustained attention to facts and to practise a greater economy of language. He also criticized Dudek's interest in abstract language and moral generalization. He reacted violently to Dudek's *Europe,* of which he wrote to Layton,

I find it bad journalism, bad poetry, and bad thinking. The frequency with which he uses abstract adjectives . . . , especially "beautiful" is frightening. And Louis is so often the naivest tourist imaginable. His "social" bearing is so hollow, his perceptions so cliché, his responses so predictable. There are occasional idioms of strength, but can I say sweet nothings about scant phrases . . . ? To say that it is the diffusest possible kind of Poundian writing would only be accurate. Set it against Olson and you see how original and true Olson is. . . .

(4 August 1955 [99])

To Souster, Corman described *Europe* as "a bad performance, embarrassing":

his sense of the sea, of Europe, of Canada, of life, is trivial and trite, as well as naive. And the writing is sloppy. To be kind to it is to be dishonest.

(5 August 1955)

Unlike Souster, Dudek never permitted Corman's remarks to have any direct influence on his writing, nor did he allow a correspondence to grow between himself and Corman. Corman's remarks about Dudek's work occur mainly in the context of his struggle with Dudek for influence over Souster and to some extent over Layton, and even when understated or qualified, they are less helpful and detailed than are his comments on Souster's work.

Wish Louis were more fortunate in Canada, but his most recent work, by all odds his best, isn't calculated to win praise in aristocratic circles. . . . He never really breaks either deep enough or free enough for me, but he has a good ear, and a good sense of poetic values, and is undoubtedly a better poet than these everlasting prizewinners.

(Letter to Souster, 13 May 1957)

... Louis, whom I respect, as he knows or should know, both as a poet and person, sounds so damn pompous not to say smug in his offhand verdicts on poetry [in *Delta* articles], on everything.

(Letter to Souster, 14 November 1958 [100])

After the dissolution of Contact Press in 1967, Dudek continued to edit and publish books in association with Michael Gnarowski and Glen Siebrasse. These books included some by inexperienced writers such as Siebrasse, Paddy Webb, Stephen Scobie and Michael Harris. They represented the kind of risk publishing Dudek had wanted Contact Press to do but included no work which in any way resembled the lyrical, "projective" or phenomenological styles which Dudek had objected to in Olson, Creeley, MacEwen, Coleman and Richard Clarke. In 1970 Delta Canada divided into Golden Dog, edited by Gnarowski; Delta Can, edited by Siebrasse; and DC books edited by Dudek and Aileen Collins. DC has continued the policy of publishing writers of rational consciousness — Marc Plourde, Avi Boxer, Harry Howith, John Glassco — and also Dudek's policy of publishing his own work privately.

Souster has spent much time since 1967 editing school anthologies — "missionary work," as he described it to Cid Corman — to replace the "pretty hopeless stuff" which "the kids have to read by and large." [101] His anthologies include *Generation Now*, edited with Richard Woolatt; *Made in Canada*, edited with Douglas Lochhead; and *100 Poems of Nineteenth-Century Canada*, also edited with Lochhead. Since 1964 he has published nine large collections of his own poems, all with commercial publishers. Some of the most recent of these (*So Far / So Good*, 1969; *The Years*, 1971; and *Selected Poems*, 1972) finally collect the many unpublished poems which his slim collections of the forties and early fifties could not accommodate.

The years 1952 to 1967 were the productive years of Dudek and Souster's association. During the early part of these fifteen years, despite profound philosophic disagreements, they exclusively kept alive the tradition of activist literary publishing which had been begun in Canada by Smith and Scott's *McGill*

Fortnightly Review and continued by Sutherland's *First Statement*. Through their magazines they attempted to keep Canadian literature in touch with the main currents of United States and western European literature and to stimulate within the country's writers and readers a respect for an experimental, innovative standard of poetic composition. Their task struck Corman as extraordinary:

People like yourself, Irving and Louis, are, in a sense heroic. You have to fight lethargies beyond our conception here.

(Letter to Souster, 23 September 1953 [102])

They shared a much larger responsibility than two or three men should have had to assume in a country of Canada's size and literacy.

For the poetry of tradition and convention—Pratt, Birney, Watson, Page, Smith—the fifties was not a "barren" decade, but Souster's statement "I always think of the fifties as an era of retreat" [103] is true from the perspective from which he and Dudek were obliged by their aesthetic principles to view it. Together Souster and Dudek "bridged a difficult time in Canadian letters," a time in which postwar political conservatism was mirrored in the strength of conservative, academic literary standards heavily influenced by Eliot, the New Critics, the Fugitives, and in Canada by the related McGill Movement and the so-called "Frygian School."

The overall achievement represented by the collaboration of Dudek and Souster is difficult to measure exactly. Certainly their publications had an effect. Authors who might not have been widely published in the fifties or early sixties but for *Contact, Delta, Combustion* and Contact Press (Mandel, Webb, Jones, Purdy, Acorn, McEwen, Bowering, Newlove, Atwood) have gone on to enjoy extensive commercial and noncommercial publication, and this has unquestionably altered the way Canadians view their country's poetry. Many of the younger writers of Souster's *New Wave Canada* have gone on to emulate Dudek's and Souster's editorial work by founding their own little magazines and small presses.

However, the literary ventures of Dudek and Souster were

most significant in the area of literary principle. Especially important was Dudek's conviction that commercial presses exist to make a profit rather than to advance literature — that they treat literature as commodity rather than art, and that he who controls the means of book production, whether commercial or noncommercial, controls the direction in which literature can move. The general acceptance of these ideas has caused not only the establishment of numerous writer-owned presses in the past decade — Coach House, Anansi, Pulp, New Press, Ingluvin, Very Stone, Weed/Flower, Talonbooks, Sono Nis, New Star, Intermedia, Missing Link, Porcepic, Valley Editions, Blew Ointment, Blackfish, Black Moss, Soft Press — but also a distinct preference on the part of many writers to have a small press serve as their principal publisher. For recent writers such as Victor Coleman, George Bowering, bpNichol and Michael Ondaatje, the small press has been not a stepping stone to commercial publication but rather a preferred vehicle for publishing their work.

Dudek and Souster also introduced to Canadian writers the principle that literature must be continually made new. In this view, mere avoidance of cliché is not enough; good writing involves in its form and content the elimination of even the appearance of the commonplace or derivative, as Pound's "MAKE IT NEW" doctrine declares. [104] Moreover, they have taught that Canadian literature must renew *itself*. Before *Contact, Delta* and *Combustion* and the attention these magazines paid to Canadian writers who were attempting to find their own modes of articulation, literary experiments in Canada had been guided by foreign examples — and only after these experiments had been certified as acceptable by foreign critics. Thus Carman used Emerson, Roberts used Keats and Tennyson, and Smith used Yeats and Eliot. A native experimental tradition within Canadian poetry begins with Dudek and Souster; it gathered strength from Dudek's belief that Canadian writing is the primary responsibility of the Canadian avant-garde magazine and from Souster's attention to new writing in *Poets 56* and *New Wave Canada*; it became firmly established in the generation of writer-editors and writer-publishers that followed their pioneering efforts.

CHAPTER TWO

Functional Poetry

True technique . . . consists in *skill in achieving a real end*, not just in making a poem. . . .

("Patterns of Recent Canadian Poetry," *Culture* XIX, 411)

Tell em to open their mouths, you want to see their back teeth, their tonsils. Tell em to say AHHH. Most Canadian poetry is written with the mouth closed. Ask them to write again when they think they've said something straight from the shoulder, no monkey business. Goddamn decoration. All icing and no cake. All cake and no meat. We want something to chew into in a poem, not just words.

(Letter to Souster, 26 November 1951)

Throughout his career, Dudek has insisted that literature must have principally a social role and must engage itself with the actual conditions and issues of contemporary life. Experimental literature consists not of exercises in pure aesthetics but of attempts towards more emphatic, effective and action-inducing uses of language. Writers are obliged to renew the language not because of intellectual or literary principle but because of society's need for language as an effective tool of analysis, communication and exhortation.

The activist aims of Dudek's little magazine and small press ventures always extended beyond literature and into gen-

eral society. When Souster first proposed *Contact* (then
tentatively titled "MAKE IT NEW"), Dudek exclaimed:

Goddamn it, it's really what Canada needs. Not only in lichechoor,
but in emotions, ideas, personalities, policies, buildings, faces, radio
programs, damn weeklies, imitations, conventions, one-track minds,
goody-goodies, there's no end to it. [1]

Two months later, after *Contact*'s name had been decided, he
wrote to Souster:

the trouble with our whole LITTLE INTELLECTUAL culture is
the completely psychotic breakup of values, where nobody shares
anything with anyone else, nobody can bear to talk to anyone for
more than five minutes. We do not even share an admiration for the
four greats of our time, YEATS JOYCE ELIOT POUND: if we did
at least that we'd have the makings of a unified culture, the basis for a
common understanding. There's been an earthquake. Can anything
be done to sew the earth together? "Sow" the earth together? At least
try to get at each other again, and make "Contact." [2]

Dudek's sense of a social duty for literature ("sewing the earth
together") had roots deep in both his life and in his doctoral research. His early poetry was strongly coloured by leftist convictions, not only about social injustice but about the role of art
as an instrument in bringing about social change. Many of
these poems had overt political messages, like "A Factory on
Sunday":

> That yellow chimney against the sky,
> . . . .
> Is a tower built for a strange god.
> . . . .
> . . . it is also the bossed bludgeon
> Of the ape-man and barbarian
> A symbol of his lust for power
> Set in the ground to stand
> In the sight of the cowed and beaten.

> Then, most of all, it has the mystery
> Of an occult Egyptian censer
> Held in the hands of priests,
> Sending incense down to the people,
> Making them bow down and pray.
>
> (*CP* 5)

Although Dudek's leftist ideas weakened once he moved to New York and came under the influence of the aristocratic values of Trilling, his sense of literature as an instrument for cultural change was sharpened by the research to which Trilling, Barzun and Neff directed him. Dudek wrote his dissertation about Carlyle, Thackeray and Dickens, all men who had used their writing to speak directly to society about itself. Of the three, Dudek preferred Carlyle, who took a crusading "stand for integrity" rather than, like Thackeray, creating "literary compromise" or, like Dickens, giving "compliance" to "popular taste."

His life's aim ... was practical and constructive. He wanted to provide a social morality, in essence the morality of all past ages, but self-imposed by men in every walk of life, until the levelling democracy should become a heroic aristocracy, a society in which the best and highest were honoured and encouraged.

(*LP* 226)

Poetry as purely aesthetic lyric and sentiment he discarded as a worthless and decadent stage of literature. ... What Carlyle looked for ... was the true poem of his age, the imaginative and passionate statement of historical truth, a work to take the pulse of the time in which he lived.

(*LP* 228)

Dudek became increasingly impressed with those twentieth-century poets (Pound, Eliot and Joyce) whose work also constituted a "criticism of culture" "in the Carlyle tradition" (*LP* 227). Speaking of the early modernist period, Dudek declared in 1963, a conception of poetry emerges which is more ambitious and original in its desire to explore total reality than poetry had ever been in the past. But this new poetry could not break through without attacking the entrenched conformities binding literature and society. And therefore the new poetry became terribly concerned with society and reality.

You see this in James Joyce, in Ezra Pound, and in T.S. Eliot. Each of these is culture-critic on a grand scale. . . . [3]

In 1950, however, this concept of literature as "a passionate statement of historical truth," as a crusading, culturally responsible activity that participates in the mainstream of the intellectual and political life of its time, was neither the dominant one in North American academies nor one which Western society itself had been interested in encouraging. There were many rival and more favoured theories of literature: the romantic, the surrealist, the aestheticist, the mythopoeic. But Dudek rejected these theories as culturally escapist and irresponsible. To him, romanticism and surrealism were products of a mental laziness which blurs the hard, substantial nature of reality.

I'm against New Romantic softness, loose mental muscles. I'm for Pound's objectivity and hardness, the personality chastened by contact with reality, and poetry hardened by fact, the stinking facts, or the seen. No mush. Well, one can experiment with surrealism, but it's so easy to get lost in that jungle. Poetry is about something, says something. [4]

Aestheticism was the result of the timid man's wish to escape from the demands of the material world into a realm of Platonic form — to avoid content and embrace "pure" design, "pure" beauty, "pure" art.

The tendency of our civilization in the past . . . has often been to move away from its relation to the real currents of life; where by "real" I mean purposeful, related to the physical basis of life, work for sustenance, economic necessity, et cetera.

Our Western civilization, therefore, has largely been falsified throughout by its *idea*-lism, its unpragmatic values, its tendency to build spiritual castles in the air. No less than a complete revision . . . is what is now required. [5]

Dudek was especially disturbed by the mythopoeic or "visionary" theory of literature, popularized by Northrop Frye in the fifties. Frye's assumption of an eternal pattern was the antithesis of Dudek's interest in the changing particulars of the present moment; further, because Frye's theory originated in Canada, it threatened Dudek's hopes of making a socially engaged realistic literature an effective part of Canadian culture. He has therefore criticized and condemned Frye almost continuously since the mid-fifties.

I revolt against a view of literature that sees it as "abstract story patterns" with "interchangeable motifs that can be counted and indexed." I oppose the tyranny of a view which claims that "mythology as a total structure, defining as it does a society's religious beliefs . . . is the matrix of literature, and major poetry keeps returning to it." I do not want to keep "returning"; I want to go forward. And I believe that literature does go forward, as human thought goes forward.

With Frye, all the meaning is to be found in the past, or elsewhere than right there on the page. . . . I want multiplicity, and actuality, and a forever-expanding field of unpredictable useful meanings. [6]

All of these theories of literature — the romantic, the surrealistic, the aestheticist, the mythopoeic — assumed one thing that was anathema to Dudek: the separation, in whole or in part, of art from life. They stressed the surface properties of art — its exotic imagery, its assonant language, its formal patterns, its plot structure — at the expense of attention either to the explicit cultural message of the work or to the cultural implications of its form. Often they glorified form isolated from significance. When they encouraged interpretation of form, they discouraged the application of this interpretation to extraliterary phenomena. They diffused the tension between art and life by transforming poetry into a commodity which the culture could comfortably absorb and patronize: the "work of art." Thus

Dudek remarks of the early culture criticism of Pound, Joyce and Eliot:

After this initial attack on existing culture . . . the first modern poets came to be accepted by the scholarly fraternity and soon were placed on a pedestal of critical adulation. Their original function was virtually ignored, just as most teachers ignore Shelley's early atheism and revolutionary activity. The mere complexity of art is more interesting because there the teacher can shine, and the student can be proven to be dull-witted.[7]

For Dudek, poetry was an instrument of social transformation.

Anyone who reads a good poem with understanding — a poem that bites into the evil, or that retrieves a truth — creates an order in himself. Every person who does this, who opposes the life-destroying forces of modern life with the assertion of full humanity as one finds it in the best poetry of our time and past times, is helping to make men free, true to their greatest capability of work and happiness.[8]

From 1950 onward, Dudek made it his major task as a writer to develop a poetic method which would defy all attempts to reduce a poem to an aesthetic object or a cultural commodity.

The death of poetry is its reduction to a purely ornamental, or "cultural" function; we must scrap the ornament and come back to meaning.[9]

He began writing in a style that contained few of the conventional characteristics of poetry: strong rhythm, rhetorical syntax, regular rhyme schemes, indirection of statement, ambiguous imagery, overt tonal patterning. Dudek carefully avoided any element which a critic or reader might be tempted to deal with separately and apart from the intellectual intent of the poem. Denotative meaning became the dominant element in his work.

Dudek deliberately tried to prevent his readers from divorcing the form of his poetry from its content or from admiring the form while ignoring the content. Unfortunately, this way of misreading literature more often originates with the reader than with the poet. Form invariably equals content and is inseparable from it. Even deliberate literary "ornament" carries a message about the seriousness of the writer, his or her fears or pretentions and the extent of the poet's commitment to a subject. That teachers and scholars have been able to isolate the form of such works as Pound's *Cantos* and Eliot's *Waste Land* almost completely from the cultural criticism they contain — so completely that the culture can "respect" the poems while continuing to practise the values those works condemn — reflects not on the weakness of the works but on the determination of the culture to neutralize literature as a force for social change. As Jean-Louis Baudry remarks, "Society . . . can tolerate and indeed appropriate every revolution 'in art' (so long as it preserves the artistic nature of the object of literary or visual production), in other words, it consigns the object back into the consumptive circuit." [10]

When Dudek attempted to counteract this characteristic of his society, he took on a responsibility that brought with it serious handicaps, risks and challenges. The first poems in his new meditative and denotative mode were the book-length works *Europe* (1954) and *En México* (1958). The apparent theory for these books followed in 1958 ("A Note on Metrics," *Delta* 5, October 1958) and 1959 ("Functional Poetry: A Proposal," *Delta* 8, July 1959). "A Note on Metrics" presents the argument that "metrical convention has nothing to do with the beauty of poetry"; "the iambic tradition" makes it "easiest to be concerned with technique." Poets must "drop the *a priori* metre out of consideration" because it encourages them to neglect responsible statement and to confine themselves to the comfortable but escapist world of pure technical accomplishment.

You thus neglect the essential music, which is that of your sounds *as they fit the content of your poetry,* and you produce for the most part an empty rattle of sounds.

(*Delta* 5, p.17)

"Functional Poetry" shows how the content of a poem can take such precedence over its aesthetic elements that all of the latter become of minimal importance except as effective media for the content. Dudek's announced aim here is to reverse "the loss of ground to prose / over the centuries / in the subject matter of poetry," to make poetry once again "capable of dealing with philosophical and metaphysical questions." This, he suggests, has been the unfulfilled and unrecognized aim of most of the great modernist writers of this century:

> As I understand it, this has been the objective
> of all modernist experiment (in English
>   since 1910, in French
>   since Laforge and Rimbaud at least)
> Call it   a return to the parting of ways
>   between poetry and prose.
>   . . . .
> . . . I go back always to the first free moderns
>   Lawrence, Aldington, Eliot (then), Pound (1915)
>   Lee Masters (yes! Sandburg too)
> for the beginning of what we need: straight language
>   and relevance to our real concerns

In the latter sections of his "prospectus" for a new poetry Dudek attempts to describe the kind of writing he hopes to see. It is to be a "poetry of exposition and discourse" based on speech and yet lifted above "shapeless pouring prose" by "rhythm" and improvisation. Such a theory definitely does not comprise, as Dorothy Livesay concludes, in an otherwise excellent essay, an "eighteenth century critical position,"[11] for most of the mechanical qualities of prose are to be avoided through the spontaneity or "straightness" of the utterance.

> Write whatever you write (for print, or letters)
>   not as prose, but as rhythmic poetry
>   (you will find the way)
>   . . . .
>   i.e. some form of improvised rhythmed speech
>   which is divided and shaped
>   by the run-on and end-stop system of notation.
>   . . . poetry having the shape of clouds.
>
>   (*Delta* 8, p. 6)

The resultant writing will be "shapely" in the way in which nature's works are shapely—through the artlessness, directness and improvised quality of their presentation. In poetry as in nature, form and content are equivalents ("the shape of clouds"); the manner of a poetic statement can never exceed its substance.

These two theoretical statements, plus *Europe* and *En México,* mark a decisive turning point in Dudek's career, the point at which he makes a full commitment to place the needs of his culture ahead of personal literary reputation and advancement. This was an extremely courageous decision in view of the predominantly aestheticist critical climate of North America during the 1950s and in view of his own proven talent for producing exquisitely rhymed and patterned verses.

In the early poems in *East of the City* (1946), *The Searching Image* (1952), *Twenty-four Poems* (1952) and *The Transparent Sea* (written 1943–54 and published 1956) Dudek's style was undefined. Poetry as plain statement and poetry as the construction of complex aesthetic objects were both clearly evident in *East of the City* and particularly in the numerous political poems. In some, technique merely served the purpose of denotation. The poet presented a consciousness that was concerned primarily with its social vision and not at all self-conscious about its words.

> I know for certain that these digging men
> nudging each other with their elbows, pushing the drill left,
> scoop clay from under the rump of profit and finance.
> Digging here and in the next street, today or tomorrow,
> something will finally happen, a bank will sag,
> a building sway like a fork on a prong;
> with shouting and throwing from side to side, the houses
> will fall into the digger's arms. The Stone Age will be gone.
>
> ("Building a Skyscraper," *EC* 44)

In others, the syntax was more complex and unnatural; the phonemic repetitions were distracting, the images strained and encumbered with adjectives. These poems were highly literary, ostensibly as much concerned with verbal construction as with social issues.

Out of the ruptured cauldron, the green factory
Whose ogre eyes gleam in the sooty night,
Railed wrists stretch over hard, broad hills,
The cold coal and straight strata, iron and steel;
The belly boils, and peal its shattering bells
Of hammers and cranes, flying their halleluyas.

("East of the City," *EC* 45)

In the majority of poems in *East of the City,* the poet's consciousness was engaged with nature rather than with society. In many of these poems, the range of the poet's response to nature, and therefore the range of the language, was limited by romantic conventions: the poet as isolated, solitary observer ("A Store-House," "Making Poems"), the poet as solitary nightwalker ("Moon," "A Shadow"), the poet as sensitive observer of trees, ferns, the moon, clouds, leaves, stars, attractive women, blossoms.

STATELY tree. See what moves
between you and me. Love.
For I have learned wisdom from trees.

("Tree," *EC* 7)

In form these poems ranged from free verse to sonnets. In the sonnets complexity of form tends to overpower meaning much as verbal complexity does in the collection's title poem. In the few poems which successfully blend formal beauty and clear statements, echoes of other poets intrude, as in the Yeatsian elements of this ending:

And I, watch how she stood
. . . .
lost in such leaves which few understand
was then no longer lonesome, cracked, and fool
as I had been before,
but I might sing and send the world to school
with such for company, to make others wise
as an old woman is, or is a child.

("An Old Woman," *EC* 9)

The central deficiency of *East of the City* is simultaneously thematic and technical. The lyrics to moon and tree appear to be from a different pen than those poems which attack the materialism of society and its callousness towards the working class. The former are largely meditative, romantic and self-obsessed; the latter are declarative, realistic and socially committed. Clearly the poet Dudek is both realistic and romantic, assertive and introspective, an admirer of nature and a critic of man. None of the technical means used in *East of the City* is, however, adequate to combine these contradictory elements.

In *The Searching Image* (1952) and *Twenty-four Poems* (1952), Dudek continued to display a large potential for technical virtuosity but no particular style of his own. Imagism, which was helping him rid himself of his conventional romantic images for natural phenomena, was now a major influence on his work; a large number of the poems open with a vividly presented visual scene— "The jewelled mine of the pomegranate, whose hexagons of honey..." (*SI* 5); "Pale from the storm's mouth / the white clouds move out..." (*SI* 2). *The Searching Image* has the wider range of technique. There are comic stanzas of *vers de societé:*

> I dreamed I was sitting with God on my knees
> while three unhappy hanged men whistled in the trees;
> a stream was flowing by of curdled blood and milk
> with a lady in the current wrapped in blood-red silk.
>
> ("Come on, Mr. Freud," *SI* 8)

At the other extreme is an early example of the meditative rhythms of "functional poetry":

> And so the emotions
>   combine into exquisite
>   counterparts of the mind and body
> when the moving principle and the natural limits imposed
>   work against each other,
>   give in, and resist.
>
> ("Line and Form," *SI* 12)

Twenty-four Poems consists mostly of highly imagistic poems in free verse. A single image presented without comment often make up the whole of the poem ("A Small Rain," "Noon," "A Morning Walk"). In "A Small Rain," the poem grows through the amplification and clarification of the original image.

> Evening. With the thin rain falling.
> A sky like moonstone.
> And here, a slender tree, at street-edge
>   one branch pointing left
>   skyward,
>   another, thin, slanting to the right
>   (*TP* XVIII)

Intermittently, these poems provide flashes of Dudek's ability to produce intrinsically arresting technical effects. In some, these effects are more distracting than enhancing.

>   ... a woman and child
> in a white wafer, standing on sepia sand,
> sways, swathed in volutes and veils of violet.
>   ("Local Colour, Night Lights," *TP* XXII)

In others, the playful rhyming of consonant, vowel and syllable serves both to reinforce and to lend complexity to the dominant denotative connections of the poetry as in these variations on $[æ]$, $[\Lambda]$ and $[\Lambda r]$:

> The pleasure I had, I had; so had the third,
> The cat; and some no doubt was reserved, in measure
> For the bird. The rest is only an abstract stir,
> Neither suffering nor having joy in my thought of fur.
>   ("The Bird," *TP* IX)

Although published two years after *Europe,* Dudek's collection *The Transparent Sea* (1956) dates mostly from the same years as his first three books. The work spans twelve years of his career, and the style is again inconsistent. However, few of these poems contain such linguistically decorative passages as do the poems in *The Searching Image* or *Twenty-four Poems,* probably because when assembling this later collection of work not previously published in book form, Dudek deliberately chose poems that fitted his new "functional" aesthetic.

Whether written in traditional or improvised verse forms, the poems of *The Transparent Sea* tend to be meditative and reflective rather than imagistic. For the first time in a Dudek collection, the consciousness expressed in the book is dominated by the reasoning process rather than the perceptual process. Dudek presents himself here as a man who worries about events, meanings and issues, rather than one who sees the visual world with especial clarity, vividness or sensitivity (as he did in *Twenty-four Poems*). In fact, *The Transparent Sea* implies a shift in Dudek's sense of the poet's identity from one who *sees* more clearly than other people to one who dares to *think* more deeply and dangerously. The poet accepts those perplexing contradictions in experience which challenge our faith in reason.

> The wise may draw what often cannot be
> built at all; or if it can be, is ignored.
> Insulted by the ear that waits for facts,
> set aside by active men,
> stalked by disease and death, as all men are,
> drowned in the apparent chaos of these times,
> artists and scholars walk their quiet ways,
> echo the pain that other men should feel, and understand,
> and make their voices heard as something seen, above all sound.
>   ("Meditation over a Wintry City," *TS* 27-28)

The Transparent Sea contains enough early poems to suggest that this alternative version of the poet's role was always present in Dudek's writing, though in the beginning it was largely masked by his interest in imagism and by his attraction to romantic convention and pure form.

The shift in Dudek's primary sense of the poet's role, reflected both here and in "Functional Verse," provided him with the technical solution that was so obviously lacking in *East of the*

City—a solution which enabled him to unite the responding and feeling self of his "romantic" poems with the critical and realistic self of his polemics. These selves become linked by meditation. The poet not only perceives phenomena, experiences emotions and reacts politically but also reflects on perceptions, experiences and reactions as phenomena in their own right. The essential subject matter of the long poems *Europe, En México* and *Atlantis* becomes not his external experiences (as it is in his imagist poems), not his subjective experiences (as it is in his "romantic" lyrics) and not his political beliefs, but his reactions to his own feelings, perceptions, beliefs, etc. The philosophical poem becomes process rather than message. As Dorothy Livesay remarks, it is no longer didactic proposition but a " consideration of possibilities." [12] The lines of the poem appear to follow the syntax of consciousness rather than the syntax of considered composition, in that they contain more appositions and phrases than clauses.

> We can't give them up, though,
> the middle classes
> of new America.
> In Provincetown, home of the Fathers,
> coming to meet the old
> out on a sand bar.

The tone becomes tentative by virtue of the addition of questions and qualifications:

> . . . the tourists
> scattered on the sand,
> . . . .
> we among them, as you said,
> "the town gets the better of us"
> But does the Atlantic
> ever to be remembered?

The poems can take surprising turns when now images appear to enter the poet's consciousness during the meditation and interrupt its apparent direction.

> Look, how the birds
> are diving against each other!
> Almost, the curved wave catches them.
> That's how we are, in the void,
>   between the now and hereafter!
>   ("Provincetown," *TS* 106–III)

This meditational mode, which combines thought and feeling in an open phenomenological structure, becomes the essential poetic of Dudek's later long poems. Its open-endedness allows a poem's development to be limited only by the duration of the poet's meditations; its use of the syntax of consciousness precludes ornamentation and admits ordinary as well as intense experience. Thus the poetic becomes "functional" not only by making possible direct expression of personal reactions but also by opening up mundane events to poetic examination.

CHAPTER THREE

Europe, En México, Atlantis

Europe (1954), *En México* (1958) and *Atlantis* (1967) are three of
the most experimental poems written or published in Canada.
Because they employ few of the established poetic conventions,
they challenge traditional distinctions between prose and
poetry. They openly invite the pejorative description "chopped
prose" which the original vers librists often encountered. In
fact, as "Functional Poetry" reveals, Dudek at the time considered this pejorative a compliment.

> "Chopped prose" is what they called
> vers libre in the beginning—
>   "Listen to the fool's reproach
>   IT IS A KINGLY TITLE!"

All three poems defy and frustrate the processes by which
poetic reputations have been made in Canada in this century.
They are much too long to be read at one sitting or to be included in trade or college anthologies. Because the individual
sections derive much of their power from the context, excerpts
but weakly represent the whole if they are anthologized
separately. In these poems, Dudek also eschews the attention-
getting devices used by his contemporaries: Layton's bombastic

rhetoric and sensational opinions, Smith's and Page's delicate fretworks of rhyme and image, Cohen's melancholy surrealism, Purdy's endearing folksiness and garrulity or Atwood's terse psychodrama. Unlike these writers, Dudek does not try to make a commodity of his personality by using poetry to project a self-image which can be loved, hated, envied or reviled by the reader.

Dudek's "functional" antidecorative and anti-imitative aesthetic dominates the expressed ideas as well as the form of *Europe*. The poem is a record of Dudek's reactions to various European cities, scenes and institutions which he visited during the summer of 1953. Although arranged chronologically, its ninety-nine sections in no sense form a narrative; the *story* of Dudek's travels is not the subject of the poem. The poet's reactions are continuous with the poem's aesthetic premises; Dudek consistently recoils from sham, hypocrisy, avarice and self-importance but warms to honesty and authenticity. *Europe* thus has a wholeness, an integrity of vision in which language and form obey the same moral view that informs the poet's opinions and judgements. This degree of integrity is seldom found in modern literature except in the work of major artists such as Joyce, Pound, Williams or Olson. Dudek understood when writing *Europe* that there can be no great art without this wholeness of moral vision in which the artist has the courage to carry out in the form of his work the aesthetic implications of his social ethic. This connection obtained for medieval man, the cathedral builder: "Norman Gothic / that did not even try to be beautiful. Only true" (*E* 43). It did not obtain for the pretentious and self-conscious eighteenth century: "Sentiment and vacuity in English art, blame it / on the eighteenth century, blame it on respectability" (*E* 45).

This theme of artistic integrity dominates the central section of the book entitled "France." Here Dudek decries imitative art that is not an extension or expression of personal belief:

> "art for art," copying the Greek forms
> shape without sense, imitating
> imitations, dramatic motion, sensuality

> for the boudoir, decorativeness
> to make room for gold, for size.
> After this, there was no honesty
> whether in art or trade....
>
> (*E* 64–65)

The turning away from authenticity and towards "corruption, *le bon goût*" (*E* 64), comes just after the building of the cathedral at Chartres: "After the thirteenth century it all deteriorates" (*E* 68).

> By the seventeenth century, the smoothies
> had learned how to cut an arch
> or a cornice with the brainless exactitude
> of precision instruments,
> and made them all alike:...
> . . . .
> (manners without meaning,
> without virility)....
>
> (*E* 69–70)

Thus aesthetics is clearly a moral subject which affects not only art but all of society — the "honesty" of trade, the sincerity of "manners," the activities of the "boudoir." Pretentiousness and precision may produce a veneer of elegance and sophistication, but they destroy the crude and unpredictable effects which signify "honesty":

> Begin with Notre Dame La Grande
> in Poitiers
> . . . .
> magnificent oval, crooked as the honest hand
> that made it,
> hand made, the rugged face, Romanesque the arches,
> old Gothic, in the side arches,
> the central round
> and the ornate sculpture, savage
> rough, plumb true, not made to be "aesthetic"
> (in Bellini you will see the aesthetic
> replacing the genuine emotion of
> Ghirlandaio, Angelico;...
>
> (*E* 68–69)

There are many crudenesses in *Europe*. Because he wants to be "an honest hand," Dudek does not bother to conceal lack of inspiration under a covering of "smooth hypocrisy" (*E* 64) or "shape without sense." Many passages in *Europe* appear commonplace; they refer to moments when Dudek was not greatly moved by his experiences but was merely recording his passing reflections. Such passages are truly "functional." They are analogous to the undecorated structural parts of a Gothic cathedral.

> It's a small world, a very small world
>> we move in,
> but it takes us by the heart
>> takes us in
> before we know it and we hate to part with it.
>
> (*E* 34)

A more important awkwardness in *Europe* arises from Dudek's inability to give up pretentious, decorative and rhetorical modes of writing. Occasionally his rhythms become artificial, as in the last five lines here, and argue a less than believable emotion.

> The Indians would have been surprised.
> A canoe is all right.
>> Or a sail on the water.
> . . . .
> But this
>> Evil of whirling knives
> . . . .
> this is devil, is contrary to GREAT SPIRIT
>> — if a ship can be that important.
> It will come to no good.
>
> (*E* 16)

Other passages have touches of formal rhetoric, which in the following example openly belie the announced theme of moving "with the rhythm of the ocean."

Let your body
move with the rhythm of the ocean,
. . . .
O let your body
rise and fall to this new river

. . . .
learn to be borne
gladly on unexhausted waves.

(*E* 26)

Most of these various awkwardnesses occur because of the
nature of the poem. Dudek appears to have had no conscious
plan when he began *Europe,* no outline of structure or plot. The
poem presents itself as Dudek's challenge to his experiences in
Europe. He records his insights whether or not they are profound or beautiful. The first fifty pages lack either intellectual
profundity or passionate feeling. At the end of the second section when Dudek sails for France, he asks,

Will Europe be any better?
Will it tell us
what we have come for? I ask the white sea
if there is life anywhere
as foaming, as glowing green, as this;
if land can possibly be, or have,
ever, all that the sea contains.

(*E* 52)

Because of its diurnal and invocative qualities, *Europe* can
properly be considered a rite poem in which Dudek works
through the process of recording his insights in the faith that he
will eventually arrive at some significant statements or some
answers to his questions. For example, while Dudek has only
banalities to offer about the sea during his outbound voyage
(sections 1 to 26), after his disappointing visit to England, he
discovers that the sea is not only his muse ("I ask the white sea")
but also the true standard by which he must assess his
European experiences.

> Although we have come far
> to see what we have seen, I do not think
>   that we shall ever equal the sea.
> History is really the study of failures,
>   the best buildings
> lack some points of proportion, dimension.
> Only the sea makes her circle perfect.
>
>   (*E* 53)

This insight leads him into the next major section, "France," which contains some of the strongest passages in the poem. It also heralds a new awareness of the sea as a major image which later gives a title to *The Transparent Sea* and a focus to *Atlantis*.

Thus the poem *Europe* develops into an ironic commentary on its title. The narrator expected to find enlightenment in Europe but instead finds superficiality, triviality and materialism.

> London, this is not what I have come to see.
> This is the present, I have seen it
>   in New York, in Toronto
> The same crowds at lunch time, the same lunch counters,
>   banks, and shopping centres.
> People, without a place, without a time but the moment, . . .
>
>   (*E* 44)

Europe, he discovers, is a "heap of ruins" populated by a tired, decadent people, worthy neither of its artistic and religious past nor of its relationship to the ocean.

> . . . all Europe is a heap of ruins
> covered over with new buildings; new voices
>   fill the air where the hammer
> chipped the rock once, the bell tolled
> serenely. We take the spray on our faces
>   like tiny tears
> from the great duct which is green and golden.
> Can you hear?
> The sea is angry, because they have deceived her
>   and lied to her.
>
>   (*E* 73)

The enlightenment he finds resides not on land but in the ocean, which is here the measure and judge of the continent, "angry" because it has been "deceived" and "lied to." Increasingly the ocean becomes the true subject of Dudek's poem.

A dichotomy between land and sea (which encompasses various antitheses such as masculinity and femininity, stasis and chaos, stagnation and fertility, human culture and cosmic process) pervades the poem and gives it strong primitivist implications. These implications dominate in the poem's most convincing passages, which include the previous example and some of the concluding sections.

> The sea retains such images
> in her ever-unchanging waves;
> for all her infinite variety, and the forms
> inexhaustible, of her loves,
> she is constant always in beauty; . . .
>
> (*E* 135)

The sea is fertility, "the globed universal belly / bulging with wombs" (*E* 22); it is art, "the only measure of music" (*E* 29); it is eternity:

> The sea has washed out
> everything I have written, the fiction of temporaneity:
> we are back with the real, the uncreated
> chaos of ocean,
> which will not stop to spare us
> a regret for all we have lost and forgotten.
>
> (*E* 133)

But Dudek also resists these implications, especially at the end of the book where many lines appear to deny the sea's relevance to man.

This was certainly beauty, but of a kind not desirable
to man, who looks for happiness, and comfort
in a world he can control.
The sea in itself is more than he can take
with any real advantage.

(*E* 136)

> ... the sea cannot be planted, is no place for cities.
>
> (*E* 137)

Here Dudek appears to contradict his own muse and to reaffirm a faith in the relationship between land and civilization which had been undermined by his European journey.

It is difficult to assess a book like *Europe* in which the poetry is so stubbornly functional and which so faithfully records the poet's search for meaning. While most of the writing is graceful and embodies, as Douglas Barbour had noted, "qualities normally associated with scintillating prose,"[1] in few passages does the poet seem to have been deeply moved by what he was writing. Only eight or nine of its ninety-nine sections reach the level of excited discovery that Dudek's own aesthetic requires ("only the power / that is married to beauty survives") or approach the melding of form, energy and function exemplified by the sea:

> to carve the line
>   positive and true
> in the smallest detail, and in the large
> harmonious with the body;
> to follow the rise and fall of the greater tide.
>
> (*E* 71)

In a collection of lyric poetry, of course, as many as nine individual poems of comparable power would make a successful book.

The outstanding passages of *Europe* (passages 19, 33, 40, 42, 50, 52, 59, 67 and 81) are concentrated in the "France" and "Southern Europe" sections. Here the usual Dudek skill in locating the syllabic music most suitable to his meaning is accompanied by a syntax that both compels the reader to hear its rhythms and implies a similar compulsion in the poet to have followed them. The best of *Europe* is represented in the following excerpt from passage 52:

> we have come into disgusting centuries   1
> where everything grows worse perpetually,   2

the sewage floating on the tide   3
    where the white wave was broken.   4
And only now   5
only now we begin to see, begin to be despising   6
viscerally, all that bad taste   7
and monastic idiocy, all that corruption   8
in man and society through 500 years;   9
only now, looking for one or two   10
objects or men, in all Europe   11
the few who work from the centre   12
wrestling with the evil before them   13
    in what they say, making the words   14
ring true to nature   15
    ("the exact word"   16
said Pope, and Wordsworth, and Boileau,   17
    and Victor Hugo of the many Squares),   18
only now, and not in France   19
    (here the fake classic persists),   20
only now we seem to turn on the foetid tide   21
    of history,   22
making for clean water.   23

                                                    (*E* 69–70)

Here subtleties of rhythm and phonemic repetition combine to give subliminal emphasis to the declarations of conviction which form the overt substance of the passage. The rhythm resembles that of excited speech and has its own idiosyncratic regularity; most striking is the fact that every line has a primary stress on its ultimate, penultimate or peripenultimate syllables. This feature gives to each line a sense of climax, and to those which are enjambed a sense of suspense as well.

The vowel and consonant patterns of this passage are quite complex, although none of these patterns (in keeping with Dudek's rejection of aestheticism) have a regularity which allows them to become the dominant element. If we concentrate our analysis on the vowels in the heavily accented syllables (the only ones in which the vowels are heard in normal speech), we see that almost every one of these recurs in another accented syllable within three lines. Thus in the opening line the [ə] of *come* recurs in the second syllable of *dis-*

gusting, while the [ɛ] of *centuries* recurs in *everything* and perpetually. The [e] of *wave* in the fourth line returns in the seventh line's *taste*. The sixth and the ninth lines are linked by the [ay] of *despising* and *society*; the seventh and eighth by the [ɪ] of *viscerally* and *idiocy;* the ninth and eleventh by the [ɪu] of *years* and *Europe*; the tenth and twelfth by the [ɪʋ] of *two* and *few*; the eleventh, twelfth and thirteenth by the [ɛ] (also found in lines one and two) of *men, centre* and *wrestling*.

A pattern of recurring consonants also contributes to the music of these thirteen lines. The key words are *worse* and *sewage* in the second and third lines. These both contribute a [w] and an [s] which also recur in many of the accented syllables that follow. These recurrences — *sewage, wave, now, see, despising, viscerally, taste, society, now, few, centre, wrestling,* etc. — weave through the vowel repetitions and amplify the rhetorical "only now . . . only now . . . only now." The consonant pattern is further supported by the occurrence of [s] and [w] in less heavily accented syllables (unlike vowels, consonants in syllables that receive tertiary or weak stress are audible in normal speech). Thus *where, white, we, idiocy, work, with* also contribute to the music of the thirteen lines.

The same consonants recur again from line 14 to the end of the passage — *what, say, words, word, Wordsworth, Squares, France, classic, persists, now, seen, history* — and are augmented by the recurrence of [n] ("only now and not in France") and [t] ("to turn on the foetid tide of history"). In syllables of primary stress these consonants often coincide with audible vowel recurrences as in *say/nature* (ll. 14-15), *Pope/Boileau/Hugo* (ll. 17-18), *France/classic* (ll. 19-20) and *persists/history* (ll. 20, 22). Occasionally they also create instances of full rhyme. The final line, perhaps to emphasize the newness of the "clean water" which it announces, has no overt phonemic resemblances to the lines immediately preceding except for the very weakly stressed [t] of *water*.

This kind of musicality directly reinforces the conscious levels of the writing, like the sound which Dudek describes in "A Note on Metrics" as an "essential music" — "that of your sounds *as they fit the content of your poetry."* The "music" does not present itself to the reader as entirely conscious or intentional.

If we drop the *a priori* metre out of consideration, all the attention must be given to the music of syllable and phrase, to the melody. Unless you have poetry in you, you cannot create such music.

Such music is theoretically the work of a "good ear," the result of having "poetry in you," of being able to select instinctively from the multiplicity of linguistic choices available the sound or syllable most appropriate to the content of the poem.

Of course, the content of such a passage derives not only from the "ideas" it expresses but also from the music we have just examined. That is, the content is equally the "ideas" and the energy, passion, commitment, sincerity which the music of singing speech projects. A prose paraphrase could never present the same content because it lacks the music. The reader finds the meaning by correlating the "ideas" and the "music" and thus participates in the composition of the poem. This process avoids the usual teacher/student relationship of writer and reader in a meditative poem; it is also the antithesis of the capitalist producer/consumer relationship in which the poem is both an aesthetic commodity and a means of propaganda. Dorothy Livesay pointed towards this aspect of Dudek's writing in *Europe* and *En México* in her article "The Sculpture of Poetry" when she remarked that their musical effect was not the aesthetic one "of onomatopoeia but a kinesthetic identification with the object seen and its flow."[2] The best of Dudek's writing in *Europe* indicates content through linguistic music as well as through denotative and imagistic expression. Conversely, in the weakest passages the music is absent. There ideas stand alone without any indication of how the poet feels about them or about writing them.

En México, Dudek's next book-length attempt at "functional verse," lacks individual passages equal in power to the most passionate lines in *Europe*, but the book is considerably stronger as a whole. *En México* begins at once with rhythms that suggest spontaneous thought. While the images appear superficially to be from an objective world, the rhythm reveals them to be thoroughly internalized: the objective is located within the subjective. The process of apprehension is now as much proprioceptive as perceptive; the poet attends to his own breath and mental rhythms as objective measures of the phenomenal world.

> A roar of sea, in constant surrender
> to sun and rain
> and palm trees opening genital limbs.
>
> By the shores where Cortéz landed.
>
> In a world of strangeness
> all thoughts run together,
> then come singly
> like those bell-birds of Vera Cruz.
>
> (*EM* 5)

Here the poet combines the elements of language — image, rhythm and denotation — to express a simultaneity of perception and response. In *Europe*, except in the best passages, perception and response were divorced; passages of externally focussed description were opposed by passages of self-conscious rational analysis. The gain in projected authenticity which Dudek achieves by the unified proprioceptive methods of *En México* is both large and striking.

Most of the passages in *En México* give the sense of suddenly opening a doorway onto intense and continuing mental activity. Several begin as though they were continuations of a state of mental excitement which has not been previously recorded in the poem.

> And where Cortéz with his men
> (their pockets full of booty)
> waded in blood, they've drained
> the lake and streetcars ride
> where he shook the Indian by the arm and cried,
>   "You have destroyed
> the most beautiful city in the world —
>   Tenochtitlan!"
>
> (*EM* 14)

Often abrupt shifts of mood occur between passages. These

shifts not only give variety and surprise to the poem but also confirm that the blank space between the passages (in the original edition of *En México* each passage occupies its own page, being positioned against the bottom margin and preceded by half a page or more of blank space) is not a void but a field of content and activity hidden from the reader.

The aesthetic standard of *En México* has also changed slightly from that of *Europe*. While the earlier book praised the spontaneous and belief-informed carving of the medieval sculptor, the reference point in *En México* is the Mexican jungle —wildly spontaneous, fecund and surprisingly orderly. Reason itself is exemplified within the jungle's primordial steam of excess and motion; in fact, the jungle becomes for Dudek a collective equivalent to Blake's "tygers of wrath." Sometimes he expresses this idea imagistically:

> Lizards chucking under the eaves.
> Vultures among the leaves.
> The comical pelican. The plunging fish.
> The coconut used as a dish.

> > (*EM* 70)

On the next page he makes an open declaration.

> Where did reason arise?
> The science of cleanness
> fastidiousness in art?
> Somewhere in this, the market, the church,
>   the commissary.
> No matter how steamy the jungle
> small leaves are perfect in detail.
>   Order remains unimpaired
> in man and in matter,
> despite all poverty, insanity, or war—
>   the jungle, in its excesses.

> > (*EM* 71)

In both modes, the language is the musical one of "felt thought," of perception and reflection transmitted kinesthetically through the whole man.

The most fascinating thematic aspect of *En México* lies in its relationship to *Europe*. In both poems Dudek challenges a landscape to reveal meaning. His search in Europe, a long civilized landscape, is frustrating and disappointing. He discovers only the loss of meaning suffered by the Europeans; the significance he sees in the ocean consistently dwarfs anything he can find onshore. Paradoxically, the primitive world of Mexico proves infinitely more pure and instructive for Dudek than all the traditions and sophistications of Europe. In the jungle, and in the people who are still connected to the elemental processes of the jungle, he finds an authenticity of purpose equal to that which he had perceived in the Atlantic's waves; "the jungle has an oceanic luxury" (*EM* 15).

> Study the way of breaking waves
> for the shape of ferns,
>   fire and wind
> for whatever blows or burns.
>
> (*EM* 68)

In Europe since the thirteenth century, form has been pretentious and insincere, but on the ocean and in Mexico life can be "simple and bare" (*EM* 78) and form "the visible part of being."

> Form is the visible part of being.
> We know, the logic of its adaptations —
> a signature of individuality.
>   an integrity.
> the end of perfect resolution —
>
> (*EM* 75)

Thus Dudek's Mexican experiences confirm his "functional poetry" aesthetic. He envisions poems that are as direct an expression of purpose as are the trees of the jungle.

> Someday we shall come again to the poem
> as mysterious as these trees,
>   of various texture,

```
        leaves, bark, fruit
        (the razor teeth so neatly arranged,
        so clean the weathered root).
        There is the art of formal repetition
        and the art of singular form — lines, lines
                like a wave-worn stone.
```

(*EM* 69)

In fact, *En México* eventually leads Dudek even further from "the act of formal repetition" to the radical proposition that all authentic motion is art.

```
            Therefore art is everything;
            but not as we imagined.
            Art is really the way of life.
```

(*EM* 76)

Throughout the book Dudek's writing follows this proposition so closely that he successfully avoids the rhetoric and pretentious rhythm that marred *Europe*. In places, *En México* tends towards the superficial and commonplace; however, these faults are not numerous. At the time of its publication, *En México* was easily the most impressive and original long poem yet written by a Canadian.

In *En México*, Dudek does not shirk the primitivist implications of what he feels and sees. Ultimately in *Europe* he termed the sea's beauty "not desirable in man"; in *En México* he proposes the jungle's "oceanic luxury" as the originating force of fertility, art, morality and worship. Again, he confronts the dichotomy between order and chaos, but now the unpleasantness of chaos is outweighed by a desire for fecundity.

```
            You may hate the jungle,
            its inimical insects, flies,
            and the chaos of growing
            everywhere at once;
            but we return for fertility
            to its moist limbs
            and vaginal leaves.
```

(*EM* 34)

The "arts" have "a beginning of adobe huts / and jungle kraals" (*EM* 7). The Mayan temple with its various intellectual, spiritual and cultural immensities has its source in a green chaos of beauty and cruelty.

> How the temple came out of the heart of cruelty
> and out of the jungle the singing birds!
>
> (*EM* 23)

In *Europe* Dudek rejected the ocean as something in which "we are not really interested . . . an empty desolation" (*E* 137), but at the end of *En México* he accepts the jungle and finds in its paradoxes a subject for contemplation.

> No matter how steamy the jungle
> small leaves are perfect in detail.
>
> (*EM* 71)

> The cumulus grows. The ocean heaves.

> Below me, the patterned fields
>   lie green, and brown, and red.
> Desert and jungle
>   around the fertile plain.
>
> (*EM* 78)

The quality of *En México* is not eclipsed by that of the longest of Dudek's major poems, *Atlantis*, published in a 154-page edition in 1967. The movement evident in *En México* away from pretension continues, but lapses into commonplace increase. Many of these lapses are related to Dudek's increasing fondness for epigram. Epigrammatic statements are an insignificant element in *East of the City, Twenty-four Poems* and *The Searching Image*, but later they often become the concluding focus of a stanza, as in *Europe's* section 23:

> No one is rejected
> from nature. That's why
>   we suffer so for our mistakes.

Sometimes, in *En México,* an entire section of a poem consists of a single epigram:

> Evil is the weft of reality!
> But the whole cloth is good, is good.
>
> (*EM* 65)

Laughing Stalks, a collection of Dudek's comic and satiric verse published the same year as *En México* (1958), contains not only numerous epigrammatic passages but a number of free-standing epigrams, and suggests that Dudek's taste for epigram developed concurrently with his interest in "functional verse." However, in *Laughing Stalks* there is no expression of the "functional verse" aesthetic; that is, none of the poems contains the subtle modulations of sound and rhythm which reveal the emotionally engaged person behind many of the observations and reflections of *En México.* In *Laughing Stalks* there is no attempt to display the poet as person in the presence of his experiences. The voice is the conventionally wry one of light verse; the rhythms and rhymes are also the standard ones of that genre:

> The verse you've read was mine of course;
> So badly read, however, it sounds like yours.
>
> ("Epigram from Rome," *LS* 93)

The central limitation of epigrammatic writing is that the full weight of the poem rests on the quality of its thought. Where this thought is clever, original or profound, as it is in several of the poems in *Laughing Stalks,* especially the parodies of various Canadian poets, the poem can be instructive and entertaining, but when the thought is slight or banal, the poem offers little. The same limitation governs denotative prose.

Dudek's interest in epigram as a form apparently prevailed throughout the period 1961–67 when he was writing *Atlantis* and eventually resulted in another semididactic collection called *Epigrams* (1975). It is quite possible that Dudek was able to rationalize the epigram throughout these years as a kind of "functional verse," inasmuch as its impersonality, its terseness and its abrupt rhymes, when combined with original thought, do contribute to a spare, almost oracular presentation. But the consistent use of epigrams limits the scope of a poem; the poem becomes "functional" only in terms of the achievement of a small objective: the presentation of an idea in a clever or arresting manner.

If one can picture the various uses of language as a continuum stretching from the most complex and multilevelled combinations in which denotation, connotation, image, rhythm, syllabic sound, metaphor and symbol work simultaneously towards a single effect, to the least complex uses in which denotation alone presents a literal, nonambiguous idea, one can see the difference between epigram and Dudek's original conception of "functional" poetry. Epigram is close to the less complex end of the continuum; the dominance of denotative meaning excludes all but the most conventional possibilities of connotative meaning, rhythm, image, phonemic repetition, metaphor or symbol. In "functional verse" denotative meaning can be dominant without being exclusive; thus in the most powerful passages of *Europe* and *En México* the writing is at a level close to the most complex end of our continuum; rhythm, phonemic rhymes and imagery all act as auxiliaries to explicit meaning. These elements give flesh to the meaning and transform it into experience. The poem communicates not an idea which can be simply denied or accepted but a man in the presence of his own ideas, a man who can no more be denied than can the existence of any "thing" in our phenomenal world. The reader becomes a participant in an ongoing experience, rather than a mere consumer of a didactic commodity.

The first 142 pages of *Atlantis* are mostly written in an epigrammatic style, but they consist predominantly of unachieved epigrams, epigrams which lack a special stylistic grace or a concluding witty shift of thought:

> The modern arts have discovered chaos,
> > they have discovered the gods.
> They have discovered only the roar of titanic power.

> (*A* 53)

Every energy is an angel.
But there is a great deal of waste in nature.
Man is perhaps an attempt at economy.

(*A* 47)

I like the sea-bottom, says God.
Man, a creature, is limited to his natural elements.

(*A* 34)

Reality is mostly what you like. Each man clings to his own
like a gimlet-eyed poet, seeing his private truth.

(*A* 118)

Time is not fixed, because it is imperfect;
  and it is perfection that all change pursues.

(*A* 141)

The universe is never finished. Evil
          is never finished. We are working
to remove it.

(*A* 86)

Chatter is like churning water,
          a formless deformation of words.

(*A* 7)

The consciousness presented here is partial; it does not include
the feeling, reacting or perceiving man. The ideas appear un-
connected to either the circumstances which originated them or
the person who experienced them. Without such a context, the
ideas become intellectual commodities, arbitrary propositions
to which the reader can extend or deny assent. They are not
internalized. They lack the compelling quality of the
passionately stated ideas in *Europe* which force the reader to
acknowledge the fact that the ideas were momentarily a spontaneous part of the poet's consciousness — that they were actual
unreflected-upon phenomena in his mind.

In *Atlantis* the implied consciousness suggests a person
who experiences few significant emotions, who reacts dully to
potentially romantic vistas.

Well, I no longer visit churches
but every day walk up and down the aisle
        of Santa Maria Novella.
. . . .

I walked three circles around the spot where Savonarola died,
and bowed before the houses of great men,
        Michelangelo, Dante, Alfieri
            (extending the metaphor over a day)
and walked home through the narrow streets
        in a kind of stupor or trance.

                                                    (*A* 57)

The poet reflects on experience apparently without being
moved by it. His own ideas do not hold him long; they come
and go in desultory succession. More often than not these reflections appear to be *sui generis*; the relevant experiences are
not indicated.

        The genius of France is comic: wit
                            the supreme art
        of wisdom, spice of truth.

        The man who had a horror of whores
                            was all right
        till he discovered he was married to one.

        In Paris you can eat very little on very little;
                or you can pay a lot and get even less.
        Un petit peu de tout.

        In making love, beauty's of no moment,
                unless you need an aphrodisiac.
        Love your wife.

                                                    (*A* 75)

    In *Atlantis* the scenes appear in reverse order to those of
Europe. They move from Italy, to France, to England. The
desultory quality of the verse suggests that these places have
lost the power to fascinate that they had for Dudek in the earlier
book. He can now look at present injustices or ancient beauty

without anger, regret or astonishment. The tone of the writing is accepting rather than protesting. Dudek finds humanity, especially the ordinary people (the raw material for any civilization), continually creative and enduring. Human beings are evil and human beings are good. Good deeds, both past and present, are as numerous and as influential as evil ones.

> Genocide is not a new thing,
> > we exterminated the North American Indian.
> The English killed off the Britons . . .
> There are no Neanderthal men!

Human beings are creatures of nature and therefore not much different from the natural order.

> Think of the more general condition of nature,
> > it will save you from hysteria
> and prepare you for the textbook facts.

> Man is a new thing. Indifferent slaughter
> > was there from the beginning.
> We have only begun to care.

> A short History of Massacres could be prepared
> in a week or two of research:
> > China, Assyria, Egypt, Greece and Rome,

> the "Story" of Carthage, of Thebes,
> > > of Peru, Mexico,
> Japan.
> > > > > > (*A* 124–25)

The prevailing ideology of political systems is relatively unimportant because only that which is suited to circumstance can endure. Like artificial rhetorical forms in language, artificial political forms, even if applied by force, will ring false and perish.

> Conquest by force is possible

> but real conquest is moral
> If there is no superior life to bring there is no victory
> or the conqueror himself may be overcome.

Thus the professed antipathies between political systems may be less important than the extent to which their goals match the real yearnings of humanity.

> The question is not whether America has liberty or whether Russia
>   has equality;
> it's what they aim at.
> The question is whether either really rejects the other.
>
>   (*A* 12)

Closely linked to this political view that all tyrannies fail, that every empire falls when "the power to survive on its own labours is lost" (*A* 36), are the professed aesthetics of *Atlantis*. Very early in the book, and immediately following the condemnation of political "conquest by force," comes a renunciation of rhetorical force.

> I want to learn how we can take life seriously,
>   without afflatus, without rhetoric;
> to see something like a natural ritual,
>   maybe an epic mode revealed,
> in the everyday round of affairs.
>
>   (*A* 13)

In its emphasis on the "everyday," this passage goes beyond *Europe's* condemnation of artistic pretension, for there the artistic models are still "exceptional" works of art and sculpture. Here Dudek consciously devotes himself to the quotidian—to the commonplace, the desultory, the banal. Art must not only be functional ("Beauty without utility becomes slack," (*A* 63); it must also seek "epic" qualities within the "simple":

> . . . A time for the artist to relax
>   a time for simple truth.
> To come back to the simple fact,
>   to humanize his art.
>
>   (*A* 128)

In addition to these political and aesthetic concerns, *Atlantis* also involves a search for the nature of paradise, or the nature of the real. In fact, the principal focus of the poem seems to be a quest for the underlying principle of life which would explain its vagaries, joys and brutalities. The poet becomes increasingly insistent that this principle can be found, like beauty, in the commonplace and in the present moment.

> . . . paradise is here or it is nowhere . . .
> In streets of nights and morning,
> and men broken by labour,
> and the mountainous loom of daylight
> > filling the dark night.
>
> > > > (*A* 89)

Paradise is found in lovemaking, in butterflies, in boxes of feathers, in hell itself, as this extraordinarily fine passage with its parody of Dante suggests:

> I shall creep in.
> I shall lie waiting.
> I shall look for a chance.
>
> There, they are waiting for us!
> Who?
> > Everyone!
> > > Oh, hurry!
>
> The butterflies are dancing (lights on the Seine)
> spilling a box of feathers.
> *Bulles Bleues.*
> Someone forgot his clothes!
> O joy!
>
> They are all running together.
> Is it love?
> Who cares!
> Yes!
> Look at the lovely banner:
> > ABANDON
>
> (I can't read)

Abandon something.
It looks like they've abandoned it.

(Don't laugh. It can happen to you.
I hope it will.)

There isn't a soul left in the city.
They're all up there.
What a celebration!

Paradise, is it?

We take our heaven in small doses.
It's safer that way, for all concerned.

                                        (*A* 98-99)

Dudek would probably consider *Atlantis* a near perfect poem. The poem corresponds almost exactly to the aesthetic and moral theories it propounds. The few very moving passages in which Dudek exerts the full range of his artistic power to display a passionately perceived situation are confined to those relatively infrequent moments when "paradise" reveals itself: the aquarium scene (*A* 31-34), the zoo scene (*A* 53-55), the Florence street scene (*A* 61), the Venus passage (*A* 106-7) and the parodies of Pound's *Hugh Selwyn Mauberley* and Eliot's *Waste Land* (*A* 128-29). These six passages have overt primitivist overtones: the shrimp is "graceful as a star, or the new moon" (*A* 33); the zoo contains

    . . . man's full nature displayed in detail:
    sloth, vigour, zest, appetite, cruelty, dirt and lust;
    as well as neatness, delicacy and care,
                            ineffable grace —
    even wisdom, even grandeur;

    and the look of suffering;

    but also beauty, function, a difficult adjustment
    that makes of living a triumph and an art.

                                        (*A* 54)

These passages echo the parts of *En México* and *Europe* which refer in a similar way to the jungle and the sea. In *Atlantis* these passages serve as keystones for the book, leading into and supporting the powerful concluding pages.

Until the very end, most of the poetry in *Atlantis* is desultory and unremarkable, like the world the poet perceives. When Dudek finds only trivia and boredom, which happens most of the time, he responds faithfully to the experience and resists all temptation to "dress" it up with rhyme and rhetoric. The six-page epilogue is the only extended exception to this deliberate blandness. Because of the extraordinary outpouring of passion at the end, even the conventional reader might forgive the poem its hitherto prevailing calm. Once again, the emotion has its source in an exceptional, "paradisal" experience, in this case Dudek's return to the sea, to the "Atlantis" of the poem's title. As in *Europe* and *En México*, the sea now appears to him as a primordial, brutally authentic embodiment of world process. Like the zoo, the aquarium and the goddess Venus, "Atlantis" contains the raw material of life and art; to Dudek the sea is the "lost continent" of life's mysteries; it embodies the universal urges towards continuity, destruction, endurance and beauty. It represents the indifferent flux which includes generosity and massacres, murder and miracles:

> . . . a wild turbulence
> of possibilities
> A spiral nebula. A sea of milk.
> . . . .
> We go into darkness, into deeper darkness,
> where all embryos are shattered.
>
> An emptiness, void of meaning,
> a signless nil
> cancelling out all mathematics.
>
> The great zero of nature, in which the little numbers flicker
> like a halftone of nazi crosses
> without significance.

(*A* 146–47)

The embodiment of "Atlantis" is the North Atlantic iceberg, a mass of

> palaces, and domes,
>   and marble capitals,
> and carvings of ivory and gold—
>   Atlantis
> shines invisible, in that eternal cloud.
>
> An architecture of contradictions and inexorable chances...
> . . . .
> ... a piece of eternity,
> . . . .
> ... its still beauty assaulted
> that knew neither time nor change.
>
> (A 148–49)

The iceberg appears to Dudek like an angel of hope in a seemingly dark and purposeless universe. It draws him not only into the music of passionate exclamation but also into the crisp images of his youth.

> There is a drop of snow on death's car.
>   A cloud against the dark mountain.
> The white of the moon.
>
> There—is reality. A white flame.
>
> I see my angel, flying over the water,
> to the blue that's like a thin gas flame around the world.
>
> (A 149)

Thus Dudek achieves his quest for the "lost continent" of meaning, truth and reality.

> There is the sea. It is real.
>
> (A 151)

Atlantis, En México and *Europe* are all adventurous poems written on the outer edges of literary possibility. They challenge the language and the universe to reveal more than they have promised.

> (Lukewarm Canadians! As if anything but the extremes
> of any ideal were worth a damn . . .)
>
> *(A 7)*

The extent to which they are all rite poems, in which the poet commits himself to the poem without knowing the outcome, should not be underestimated. All three are voyage poems into distant lands and distant possibilities. In all three Dudek makes writing an act of sympathetic magic. He trusts that his questions will be answered if he explores the medium of language.

> One could not write a poem waiting for the train to start.
> But once in motion, well in motion
> how is it possible not to begin?
> . . . .
> Travel, to and from (the place does not matter)
> the Ding an sich in a mirror —
> Let it speak!
>
> *(A 3)*

This commitment to "let it speak" results in many pages of trivial, uninspired observations and reflections. However, these are redeemed not only by a few great poetic moments — *Europe*'s Chartres passage, the *Atlantis* "Epilogue" — but also by the overall fidelity to the proportions of human life which the poems preserve.

Europe, En México and *Atlantis* are thus documents of non-inspiration as well as inspiration, of the struggling, searching man as well as that man in his occasional moments of empassioned enlightenment. In this documentation of the diurnal reflections of the poet they resemble Andy Warhol's documentation of aimless lives or, even more, Proust's accounts of the banal particulars of the cloistered self. In fact, Dudek's comments on *A la recherche du temps perdu* in his *First Person in Literature* tells us a great deal about his hopes for his three long poems. Proust's novel, says Dudek, depicts the things of life "in great detail," gradually revealing them as "illusion and self-deception."

If that were all there was in Proust, however, there would be no eternity in his novel. It would not be the immortal work it is. Caught in the midst of illusion, like dreamers in the dark internal caverns of the psyche, he finds a few rare and exceptional experiences in his life, a few moments which are not ephemeral like the surrounding mists and deceptions, but intuitions of permanence beyond time and change.

(*FPL* 43)

The kind of universality he gives us in the novel . . . might be called transcendental realism, since it is realism, with all its reductive and negative descent into the particulars of life, but at the same time eternalized by flashes of transcendent experience. . . .

(*FPL* 45)

Predominantly mundane experiences and reflections briefly and abruptly redeemed by unexpected flashes of "transcendent experience" seems unarguably to be the pattern of Dudek's three major poems. It is a pattern which sacrifices the conventional pyrotechnics that guarantee success for contemporary writers. It consciously risks boring the reader in order that the writer's portrait of the self and the world will have the greatest possible accuracy and integrity.

Atlantis, En México and *Europe* all confirm Dudek's fidelity to his moral vision. Art and life, to Dudek, are inseparable aspects of a single entity: "Art is really the way of life" (*EM* 76). A poet's moral vision must not merely be the same as his theory of art; it must *be* his theory of art. If pretension is evil in life, it is evil in art; so too with hypocrisy, self-aggrandizement, the use of force, the repression of unflattering detail. Dudek demands of art the same candour, the same admission of failure, the same acceptance of process, the same probity as he demands of man and society, or as he witnesses in what he believes are the greatest works of civilization and nature. In the jungle, in the ocean, in the medieval cathedral, the joints and flaws and commonplace elements that are typical of all process show. Aesthetics are an extension of moral vision. This belief, which has been a prerequisite to most of the great art of the world, is seldom respected in Canada where writers have usually struggled to achieve competence rather than greatness. Thus Dudek's work has not been intelligently or sympathetically received. Yet his work is courageous precisely because it sacrifices popularity in order to strive for something remarkable. Dudek is one of the few Canadians who have dared to reach for a place among the best contemporary writers or risked the hazards of authenticity which they have routinely confronted. He is also one of the very few who have openly fought against the trend towards making literature an acceptable commodity and the tendency of writers to make commodities of themselves by deliberately constructing public images that eclipse their actual writing. Dudek's embrace of routine, casually observed or minimally felt events as the materials of poetry, his use of understated, prosaic, nonrhetorical language, together with his image of himself in *Europe, En México* and *Atlantis* as an exemplary rather than an authoritative thinker, have been extraordinary landmarks in the struggle to salvage literature from the commercial world of commodity fetishism and restore it to the functions of testimony and process.

CHAPTER FOUR

The Red Truck

You can go through a red light but you can't go through a red truck.
(Dudek, "New Epigrams"[1])

Louis Dudek's first important scholarly work was his doctoral thesis, *Literature and the Press*, written during the late 1940s and early 1950s, published in microfilm in 1955 and in book form jointly by Ryerson Press and Contact Press in 1960. The book is marked by the same anger at established taste and commercial publishing that informed his essay "Academic Literature" (1944) and his letters to Souster during the 1952 founding of Contact Press. The tone of *Literature and the Press* is undoubtedly influenced by Pound's various cultural and economic works and is unusual among Dudek's entire body of scholarly writing for its shrillness. Dudek begins by deploring the "devastating" effects on literature of "the mechanization of printing," the "usurious motivations of modern society" (*LP* 9) and the consequent "precarious position of literature" "in the mass communications society of the future" (*LP* 12). In the chapters that follow he analyzes the parallel post-Renaissance phenomena of expanding literacy and growing technological capability in printing, and charts the corresponding development of the newspaper, the popular periodical and the best-selling book. His thesis is that the commercial forces that directed this development "barbarized" literature by publishing exclusively for mass taste.

The popular might, and ought to be, the best, but it cannot within a system whose main drive is for quick quantity production and profit. It is the machine and the profit motive — excellent both for the multiplication of goods for physical consumption — that deteriorate quality in the products of the imagination. And the danger of the process to every civilized activity is such that the structure of material abundance can be nullified and made worthless by the barbarization and subjugation that it involves. Within the machine and money-profit system, the survival of civilized arts and literature can be maintained only in areas where neither quality production nor money play a leading role.

(LP 120)

In the final chapters Dudek surveys in detail the publishing lives of Dickens ("Victorian Best-Seller"), Thackeray ("The Literary Compromise") and Carlyle ("The Stand for Integrity") as representatives of the three choices open to the literary man in an industrial and commercial culture. He finds the work of Dickens, and to a lesser extent that of Thackeray, severely damaged by the pressure to popularize, and the life of Carlyle damaged ("closed in ever-greater bitterness and disappointment," *LP* 218) by his refusal to popularize. What remains to our own time is Eliot's "dissociation of sensibility" — "a schizoid opposition between the general reader and the writer of the so-called 'avant-garde'" (*LP* 138), an "intellectual minority which holds out against . . . commercialization" (*LP* 139). Dudek's recommendations for redressing this situation are few, and again, extreme. His final paragraph is as hyperbolic as any in the book:

we are passing now through a time of erosion in literary values worse than any which can be recalled in western civilization (darker than the barbaric invasions of the fifth century); and this destruction threatens, in a period of mass cultures and highly organized power, to become permanent. Whether we can stop this advance into a total mass-communications society is the question for our age.

(LP 238)

Overall, *Literature and the Press* is a strident, provocative, but unsatisfactory example of culture criticism. Dudek's discussion of the close correlation between technological and cultural change is weakened, like that of his rival media critic Marshall McLuhan, by a confusion of coincidence and cause. His argument that mass audiences were created by long-print-run technology contains little evidence to prove that this technology was not created to meet the needs of an already existing mass audience. His complaint about the neglect of serious literature in our culture does not take into account the possibility that serious literature has always had a minority status, but against a changing background of popular literature — the oral tradition in pre-Renaissance times, fugitive ballads and sermons in the sixteenth and seventeenth centuries, mass circulation books in later times and television in our own. Further, his book reflects very little faith in the imaginative power of artists to survive, the power which Dudek himself was to exhibit effectively in his magazine and small press publishing. In particular *Literature and the Press* shows little faith in the power of artists to turn technology to their own purposes, to use small-scale technology to supprt "guerrilla" art in a relatively clumsy large-scale culture. The contrast in this regard between Dudek and McLuhan is instructive. In *Understanding Media* McLuhan has the wrong values — those of the mass culture — but the right solution — the decentralization of cultural power through open access to the ubiquitous "cool" media. In *Literature and the Press* Dudek has the right values — those of the intellectual minority — but the wrong solution. He fails to see how technology can liberate as well as enslave.

It is difficult to guess what Dudek's hopes for this book were when it was published commercially in 1960. His clarion call for an abrupt reversal of the direction of cultural forces was not only unrealistic but also contradicted his own quiet attempts during the period 1951–60 to transform the Montreal and Canadian literary scenes from within. Its shrillness is out of keeping with the pervasive moderation of most of his subsequent writing, and stamps the book as a product of his youth and his close contact with Pound. The tone of his critical work since *Literature and the Press* has been calm, considered and well balanced, although he has continued to champion the values of an embattled elite struggling against ignorance and mass taste. The focus of his later work has been confined to Anglo-American modernism and Canadian modernism. His methods have been more textual and literary than the largely sociological ones of *Literature and the Press*, although his view of literature as an aspect of social and intellectual history, and of modernism in literature as a consequence of the growth of science and industrialization, has remained the same.

The impact of science on the poetic imagination is of course the issue. The effect of rational empiricism on belief in poetry has been twofold: it has damaged belief by denying its ground in reason (medieval man was as confident of the ground of faith in reason as science is today); and it has cut off morality, aesthetics, and all other questions of judgment from any supposed transcendental source of validity. The result on the first count has been to spread an unpalatable superficiality throughout our religious beliefs, the kind of superficiality and optimism one finds in the nineteenth century poets, or today in neat, modern, gailylighted churches. The result on the second count had been to spread a havoc of eclecticism and nihilism in various degrees throughout life and literature, leading some to brilliant leaps of reconstruction, Nietzschean, Lawrencean, Gidean, Poundist, or what not. [2]

This later work, with its more fully integrated cultural and literary approach and its implicit acceptance (rather than condemnation) of the difficult social context of the contemporary artist, constitutes Dudek's primary contribution to criticism. In comparison to this work, *Literature and the Press* appears very much preliminary.

A number of his essays, including "The Significance of Lampman" (1957), "Patterns of Recent Canadian Poetry" (1958), "E.J. Pratt: Poet of the Machine Age" (1958), "The

Transition in Canadian Poetry" (1959), and "Literature in English" (1967), argue a specific interpretation of the evolution of Canadian poetry from the Victorian period to the present. In this interpretation, "a failure to *think*"[3] is the hallmark of a generation of mid-nineteenth-century British, American and Canadian poets for whom "the Victorian imperative to see the bright side of God, Nature, and Man"[4] was stronger than any urge to attend to the implications of science for the poetic imagination. In Canada, Carman and Roberts are the inheritors of "the philosophical religion of romanticism, the Unitarianism of Coleridge, and the idealism of German philosophers," a tradition which had become "strengthless in the face of geological and biological science." If Dudek had followed here the premises of *Literature and the Press*, Carman and Roberts would have also been criticized as betrayers of literature to the pressures of popular belief.

For Dudek, the important nineteenth-century poets in English are distinguishable from other poets by being truth-demanding rather than escapist; pessimistic rather than optimistic; bitter rather than joyful. Among Canadian poets the only figure who qualifies is Lampman.

He is the only poet in Canada before 1900 who possesses the significant ground-tone of all valuable poetry in that period. Before the onset of the modern movement, whether in the "terrible sonnets" of Hopkins, or the stoical world-despair of Housman, or the philosophical pessimism of Hardy or of Robinson, a dark Melancholia reveals itself as the sign of earnestness and genuineness in the more important poets writing in English before 1910; facile optimism, following the Victorian imperative to see the bright side of God, Nature, and Man, is to be found in the lesser poets everywhere, in Stevenson, and in Lanier, as in Carman and Roberts. Lampman differs from his Canadian contemporaries as the only poet in Canada who belongs in spirit to the company of Hardy, Robinson, Emily Dickinson and Housman, not that of Alice Meynell and her friends. [6]

For Dudek the beginnings of modernism lie in the failure of the nineteenth century to modify the optimism and idealism of Rousseau, Hegel, Coleridge and Wordsworth; to accommodate the increasing power of cities and the increasing dehumanization of city life, or to confront the findings of the new sciences. The convictions of the romantic movement become "the complacencies of the popular romantic formula." [7] Lampman signals the beginning of Canadian modernism by turning partly away from this formula and towards "political and human facts."

He is the only poet of the Group of '61 who looked sharply at the political and human facts of our life. As a convinced socialist, a Fabian, he viewed politics critically. . . . [8]

More remarkably, in Dudek's view, Lampman is not only a proto-realist but also a hesitant Arnoldian culture critic:

he takes his place as the first fundamental critic of our culture and our political life; but again his failure to carry these ideas to their specific conclusions is the defect of these poems ["dealing with the city, with social questions, and with ideas"]

While "his nature poetry presents a pastoral view of nature, too perfect and pacific to be true," in his city poetry "he is a realist; that is, he reports the fact as he really knows it." [9]

In "The Transition in Canadian Poetry" and "E.J. Pratt: Poet of the Machine Age," Dudek argues that the next stage in Canadian modernism was the complete repudiation of romantic pastoral proprieties in favour of direct expression of Darwinian brutality, without (unfortunately) any complex moral analysis of this brutality. This stage is reflected in the poetry of Robert Service and E.J. Pratt. Both express the "impersonal cruelty of nature, . . . the conflict of species, . . . [the] brute nature lurking in the heart of man" but both resolve these elements simplistically, Service "in absolute contradiction: 'For I know that the whole for good is planned'" and Pratt by arbitrarily asserting "The path lies through Gethsemane." [10] Holding Pratt to the criteria of "fact" and "realism," Dudek says,

The Christian message, Love, without theological justification, may be there as a final closing ineluctable choice; but it is not derived from the facts; it runs counter to all the facts.

Despite this limitation, Pratt completes Lampman's vision of urban industrial man, expressing "through his very metrics and his personality the beat of pistons, the metallic clangour of wheels, and the apparently unreflective energy of matter." [11]

Dudek's history of Canadian modernism continues with A.J.M. Smith, F.R. Scott and A.M. Klein, who achieve "a naturalness of style in the colloquial vein." [12] Dudek now sees Smith and Scott not through Marxist eyes as merely "blueblood" artists engaged with "word-patterns," as he did in his 1943 essays, but in a broader historical perspective, as examples of the culmination of the reductive emphases of early modernism. He no longer looks upon their work as an "establishment" to be overturned, but as a necessary transitional stage in which the early modernist aims — to rid poetry of trite emotional attitudes and their accompanying imprecision of diction and imagery, to replace traditional imagery with contemporary "realistic" imagery and to purge poetry of superfluous words — are accomplished. Dudek notes the cryptic quality of Smith's and Scott's poetry:

more laconic still, so allusive in fact that the intellectual premises now remain unstated, the dry austere poems of F.R. Scott and A.J.M. Smith are the first small bitter fruit of the tree of modernism in Canada. [13]

Their work is "small" and preliminary. It constitutes only the first wave of modernism in Canada, a wave which clears the way for a second wave to build new "larger" work on foundations uncluttered by vague thought, conventional language and romantic imagery.

After Scott, Smith, and Birney, the impulse of Canadian poets has been to break through the zero point of negation (the prickly pear of the Hollow Men) toward some passionate rediscovery of a visionary, or a rational, or a sensuous affirmation of larger life. [14]

In these same articles Dudek sets forth his own criteria for good modernist poetry. Poets must first of all be intellectually immune to the deliberate irrationality of the mass culture.

The failure to *think*, and a signal success with poems that require least intellectual complexity, is in itself a clear sign that the waters of thought have become badly muddied. [15]

Secondly, they must attend to secular, factual "reality," to economic, sociological and sexual particulars—"to some individual radical secular approach to life, some grasp of the realities, whether tragic or hopeful, which stands in contrast to orthodoxy and to the morality of the past." [16] They must accept that "true technique... consists in *skill in achieving a real end*, not just in making a poem." [17] Thirdly, they must use the actual language of their time, in Canada "language... as Canadian voice and rhythm, not as English metre." [18]

... the language of common speech is the modern touchstone, and in Canada it amounts to the assimilation of poetry to local reality. [19]

Dudek's first criterion, "the ability to think," relates to the rationalist bias that pervades all his poetry and criticism except *Literature and the Press*. This rationalism expresses itself in the discursive and epigrammatic passages of *Europe* and *Atlantis*, in his collections of epigrams, and in the evenhanded and moderate tone of his most partisan essays. His appraisals of his fellow Canadian poets are usually balanced and antithetical.

The virtues of these poets [George Walton, R.G. Everson, Goodridge Macdonald] lie in the intelligent comment of an older generation on the passing crisis. Their defects are in technique, which creaks and relapses into mechanical outworn rhythms. [20]

These poets [Roy Daniells, Wilfrid Watson, Douglas Le Pan] may be inclined to heaviness and dullness. They are also among the most intelligent of the poets, knowledgeable, well-bred, inner-directed gentlemen. [21]

The metrics and the form of Pratt's poetry are about as anachronistic as his extinct dinosaur Tyrannosaurus Rex, but they have been resurrected to take part in a great moral battle of the present. . . . [22]

In Klein, as in Irving Layton, . . . this freedom with language leads to a certain barbarism of idiom and vocabulary; but the result is in general authentic poetry of time and place. [23]

This balanced structure also appears frequently in his epigrams and usually, as in the "red light . . . red truck" epigram which heads this chapter, emphasizes the futility of extremist action. "The road of excess leads," for Dudek, not to wisdom but to a red truck, to mangled bodies, or "to the nuthouse" (*Ep* 14).

Descend into chaos, but keep coming up for air.

(*Ep* 11)

A revolution is a good thing if it doesn't succeed.

(*Ep* 1)

The life of some artists is like a road race in a powerful sports car, that leaves the highway littered with the mangled bodies of women and children.

(*Ep* 9)

Extreme commitment to an idea, even to an idea as important as the social or cultural role of literature, can destroy one's ability to further that idea.

Literature has a social purpose, but the writer taken up with it may renounce writing altogether.

(*Ep* 1)

This insistence on being reasonable and moderate in one's convictions, of being balanced and temperate in the expression even of one's core beliefs, often leads Dudek to hold two contrary ideas simultaneously, and even to question rationalism itself as a sufficient approach to reality.

Whatever happens by chance happens also by design, because everything happens by chance, and everything happens by design.

(*Ep* 15)

Education is the greatest obstacle to education.

(*Ep* 25)

Unlike Blake, Dudek is not trying to reconcile these opposites but to pick a median way between them. Neither chance nor design is sufficient by itself; by implication neither intuition (to apprehend chance) nor reason (to perceive design) can be fully trusted. This particular paradox, which questions the sufficiency of rationalism, is central to Dudek's work and is especially important in his aesthetics. In art, the rational must be balanced against the phenomenal, ideas against images, abstractions against particulars.

The right proportion between abstract ideas, or intentions, and the concrete presentation of realities is what we expect in any successful work. These things are so combined that the richness and ambiguity that pertains to concrete presentation — the action of a play or a novel, the images of a poem — are given direction and held in control by the general ideas; and neither is the work impoverished by too narrow a purpose, defined by abstraction, nor is it allowed to sprawl and lose itself in a vague and wandering chaos of particulars. [24]

Nonrational elements here are for Dudek clearly irrational, must be curbed by rationality just as rationality itself must be tempered by excess.

Art is a moderate kind of madness. A mild excess of some kind, an internal upheaval, makes a man write *Finnegans Wake* or *The Remembrance of Things Past*, or *The Cantos*. [25]

This balance between the rational and nonrational has not always had the best effect on Dudek's own poetry, as he himself has observed.

I'm for . . . the poem that is highly structured in terms of the language and the images in it. I don't know how closely I myself have kept to this line because I think there's another side to my poetry, an interest in ideas, in the philosophical content of poetry; and the philosophical, contemplative content probably runs counter to the concrete or imagistic. So there's an incompatibility. [26]

Nevertheless, as his most recent poetry testifies, Dudek has continued to work with this "incompatibility" and to seek new combinations of ideas and particulars which will produce the poem that can, as he once advised the present writer, "pack a wallop with a meaning." [27]

> "I hate all laws" say the young and foolish
> and the roads are littered with bodies
>
> Like sex, an amusement park
>   rigged for catastrophe
>
> Like driving a car without steering
>   ("Continuation I" [28])

Dudek's commitment to reason underlies his criticism of Northrop Frye and Marshall McLuhan and his reservations about Ezra Pound. Originally, Dudek was attracted to Pound because of his connection with the Imagist movement, which represented the particularist, nonrationalist aspect of modern poetry.

The Imagists were important to me personally from a very early time, even before I came in touch with the *First Statement* people, Layton, and Sutherland. And these Imagists were Hilda Doolittle — H.D. — especially, and Richard Aldington.... And Pound also.... Imagism, for years, let's say for twenty years after this time of *First Statement*, was in all my teaching.... [29]

But in later years Dudek rejected Pound's interest in concreteness, in collage, ideogram and documentary materials as a failure of "clear abstract ideas." Insisting on both sides of the abstraction-particular paradox, Dudek argued that "there must be abstract ideas and there must be ideas in things: it's the proportion between them that remains the real issue for poetry."

"No ideas but in things"... is an idea borrowed from Ezra Pound. And he learned it from Ernest Fenollosa.... Ezra Pound ruined his Cantos with this idea, by making his poem a mere avalanche of concrete things, samples, without giving the reader much help in connecting these "things" together with clear abstract ideas. It's still a magnificent poem, very vivid and suggestive of multitudes of meanings; but it lacks the proportion between connecting ideas and multifaceted realities that communication now demands. It pretends to be an epic with a coherent thought, but has no coherent thought either in the parts or in the whole. [30]

In a larger sense, Dudek found Pound guilty of attempting to create "pure art" without any intellectual context or support from abstract ideas. He accuses Pound of making such art a substitute for religion and civilization. For Dudek, civilization requires "interesting ideas" as well as a "hunger for life." [31]

Ezra Pound would have us worship pure art, as a kind of religion, for the sake of civilization. He was a very angry man who partly understood the problem. He had no conception of how to make an art available; or how to reconcile the philosophical and religious problems underlying it. Pure art is art trying to stand without any religious support. That is not possible. [32]

These remarks about Pound cast an interesting sidelight on Dudek's own long poems, especially *Europe* and *Atlantis*, which were undoubtedly written with Pound's *Cantos* in mind. These poems frequently follow Pound's dictums and create a collage of various images, events and documents. However, Dudek adds to this an interpreting consciousness that places the particulars of life within a clearly defined moral and intellectual (i.e., "religious") context. This makes his poetry something other than "pure art." Where Pound may indeed fail by being not "available" (i.e., readily understandable), Dudek's work often risks failure in the opposite direction—by being overly available through banality and redundance.

Whereas Dudek had some reservations about Pound, he totally condemned the work of Pound's "Black Mountain" inheritors: Olson, Creeley and Corman. Olson and Creeley's adaptation of Pound's ideogrammic structure into a sequence of perceptions related only by association ("ONE

PERCEPTION MUST IMMEDIATELY AND DIRECTLY LEAD TO A FURTHER PERCEPTION"[33]) was to Dudek an abandonment of all semblance of a rational context. Corman's development of imagism and understatement into a new form of minimalism impressed Dudek as an abdication of the responsibility for thought. To Dudek all this work was extremist and "eccentric" because it failed to balance the primitive with the rational and because it implied a rejection of the linear growth of human culture and civilization. In Dudek's view, "eccentricity" was a severe limitation: he remarks in "Patterns of Recent Canadian Poetry," "I think no great art is eccentric, although it must be original."[34]

Dudek attacked Northrop Frye for his excessive abstraction, for his reliance on the irrational mind and for his extremism. Frye's preference for mythology over actual experience as the raw material of art offended Dudek because it emphasized abstractions rather than particulars and because it replaced "factual" reality with archetypes. Dudek believed that art must retain a balance between a public and a personal focus as well as a balance between ideas and particulars.

The word myth . . . recalls the counter-movement in modern poetry, the principle that is always opposed to the simply personal and subjective. Myths are the extreme antithesis of the individual self, they are the gods and eternal conceptions by which we universalize and depersonalize our world.

(*FPL* 66)

He rejected Frye's "visionary view of literature" which claimed that "some . . . special revelation, and not the light of common day, is the truth about life and art."[35] And in "Northrop Frye's Untenable Position" Dudek also argued that Frye's archetypal interpretation of literature was an "attempt to relegate the content of literature to the status of irrelevant 'convention.'" Dudek obviously believed that Frye's approach would deny the writer any Arnoldian role as cultural custodian or culture critic.

The suggestion that literary archetypes might exist in some kind of social subconscious, accessible to the masses or to the naive artist but not to the conscious individual, offended Dudek perhaps more than any other aspect of Frygian theory. For this hypothesis implied that the literary imagination was not part of the rational consciousness, as Dudek believed, but was outside the individual writer's conscious control. He summarizes Frye's argument with some sarcasm.

"The central myth of literature broke in on Dylan Thomas suddenly at a certain stage of his development"; thus the poet becomes significant to the critic, as one possessed by a Platonic reality over and above the rational and sensible consciousness of men, but he is not himself a useful thinker, . . . and each poet, as the critic's guinea pig, provides only a partial illustration of the archetypal plan. . . .

. . . there is no work of literature, popular trash or masterpiece, that Professor Frye cannot equate to some item of the archetypal system. [36]

From the mythopoeic point of view the babble of psychotics would make better poetry than the writing of sane people.

(*Ep* ii)

In the work of Marshall McLuhan, Dudek also found elements of irrationalism and primitivism similar to those he had rejected in Frye. However, McLuhan, with his *The Gutenberg Galaxy* (1962) and *Understanding Media* (1964) was also in direct competition with Dudek as a media critic (Dudek's *Literature and the Press* was published in 1960), and the spectacular commercial and critical success of McLuhan's books must have especially galled Dudek because McLuhan's purposes were so nearly opposite to his own. McLuhan approved the replacement of typography by electronic media whereas Dudek lamented it; he celebrated the growth of mass taste into "the global village" whereas Dudek deplored it; he debunked a linear view of history whereas Dudek relied on it. Dudek's epigrams concerning McLuhan are notably strained.

When you read McLuhan you must admit that audio-visual communication might perhaps be better.

(*Ep* 4)

McLuhan has written some pretty good science fiction.

(*Ep* 27)

Dudek began attacking McLuhan's lack of rationality as early as *The Mechanical Bride* (1951). In *CIV/n* no. 3 he wrote that McLuhan's work was "an accumulation of facts straining toward a generalization."

The issue in modern culture calls for an entirely different treatment — disentanglement, clarification, plain good sense. We need a return to sanity, not to fly to some novel kind of insanity.

In 1966–69 Dudek reviewed a number of McLuhan books in the Montreal *Gazette*. In "Marshall McLuhan Defined" he accused McLuhan of praising "mediocrity" and commented, "Only the resistance of the individual stands against this flood of mediocrity, just as the individual has always resisted the world's evil." [37] To Dudek, the issue between himself and McLuhan was as clear cut as the central issue in his own *Literature and the Press*. It was the conflict between the insanity, mediocrity and "appalling uniformity" of mass taste and the enlightened vision of the Carlylean hero. In explaining and celebrating the new electronic media, McLuhan seemed to be abetting democracy's tendency towards uniformity of values.

Its one law for man is pleasure, or "standard of living"; the economic motive of profit makes this last conclusion necessary, since pleasure is the lowest common denominator of all commercial goods, and therefore all other values give way before it. Since all men are politically equal, all competing in the economic race — in what Carlyle calls the "insane scramble" — they are soon reduced simply to pleasure-seeking animals. An appalling uniformity settles over the social scene.

(*LP* 224)

In "McLuhanism in a Nutshell" Dudek accuses McLuhan, again sardonically, of encouraging irrationality and social homogeneity and of betraying man's cultural heritage:

all that we've been trying to inculcate into the young for centuries, all that the wisest men have defended, is now being discarded as the obsolete product of individualism. It was only the product of the printed book, and the printed book obviously is finished.

He quotes some of McLuhan's remarks to suggest that they imply approval of demagogic manipulation.

"The public, in a sense of a great consensus of separate and distinct viewpoints, is finished. Today the mass audience can be used as a creative, participating force." Demagogy thus replaces critical intelligence.

For Dudek, culture is precisely "a consensus of separate and distinct viewpoints" with "aristocratic" or elite viewpoints dominant among them. The mass audience is sentimental, banal, unperceptive and intellectually lazy. He remarks in "Art, Entertainment, and Religion,"

the elite . . . have more interesting ideas. The great majority of mankind are made groggy with bad religion and bad morality; they have never examined these things. Hence their soap operas and grade-D films, soaked in sentimentality and phoney moralism. The literature of the elite is sounder in ideas. It may be sceptical or searching, cynical, satirical, or mystical, as the case may be; but it is not slobbering over foetid outworn conceptions and beliefs. [38]

Dudek charged McLuhan with encouraging the mass culture's attempts to further anaesthetize an already groggy people and with substituting "a cloud-cuckooland of irrationality, irresponsible Zen, and vague dreams of Green Pastures" for clear intelligence and sound ideas. McLuhan "has forgotten everything that matters"; "his message is a threat to our common humanity." In this quarrel, Dudek successfully avoids the stridency of *Literature and the Press* and asserts his rationalist position with renewed clarity.

Personally, I prefer Erasmus: "What is the proper nature of man? Surely it is to live the life of reason. For reason is the peculiar prerogative of man." [39]

Dudek consistently exempts his publishing partner Raymond Souster from rationalist criticisms. Indeed, Souster's lack of academic sophistication, his limited knowledge of world literature, his anti-intellectualism, appear to have engaged the entire rationalist-realist paradox in Dudek rather than antagonizing one part of it. Dudek's remarks on Souster's anti-intellectualism are quite different in tone and intent to those on the irrational elements in Frye and McLuhan.

He [Souster] is anything but intellectual or ideational. For him, the modern formula seems to read: "Let thinking be. If everything is that bad—and it is—let's live!" He demonstrates the emotions of a humane, sympathetic social being, in the midst of social depravity, of political corruption and war, without any search for underlying ideas.

Instead of asking Souster to strike a balance between factual particulars and abstract ideas, he implies that Souster's realistic or "sensuous" qualities make up for his failings as a thinker.

His method is intuitive, anti-intellectual, secula [sic], . . . fundamentally sensuous and emotional. Since he is a poet the result is poetry of our time, free of illusion, of self-deception, yet palpitating with life.[40]

In the framework of Dudek's survey of modernism, Souster's suspicion of ideas represents an exaggerated rejection of Victorian values; the Victorian abuse of ideas leads to the rejection of all ideas. Dudek does not view this as an illogical or Pyrrhic act. He can sympathize with Souster's use of everyday subjects and images and of everyday language because these elements are characteristic of his own poetry.

It was not until Layton appeared, and Souster, and myself that what was "political" before became truly Canadian and realistic modern poetry; and the language corresponded thereto as Canadian voice and rhythm, not as English metre.[41]

Dudek's association with Souster is an outstanding example of how his commitment to two opposing values in poetry—concreteness and economy of images and culturally significant intellectual commentary—could allow him to champion vastly different kinds of writing. Where other poets were concerned, these split values often caused him to waver in his support, as it did in the case of Layton, whom Dudek described as both "authentic" and "barbarous," or of Anne Wilkinson, whose work he termed both "tense" and "undisciplined."[42] In some cases, this split caused him to take radically contradictory stances. For instance, he rejected Victor Coleman for publication by Contact Press, and characterized his work, together with that of other *New Wave Canada* poets, as a "messy sort of doodling"[43]; and yet during the same period he proposed Coleman as a new editor of the press.[44] He also wavered in his evaluation of the Vancouver writers associated with *Tish* magazine. Some of these writers were included in his blanket condemnation of *New Wave Canada;* in a 1967 review Dudek called George Bowering's work "light and flimsy" and offered the advice: "One must get beyond the trivial object to some kind of significance."[45] Yet he also wrote in 1967, "the main line of continuing modern development (in Canadian poetry) runs through Scott, Souster, Purdy—and at present centers clearly in the activity in Vancouver";[46] he expanded this view in a 1978 interview with Marion McCormick:

Tish is important because it imported into Canada a kind of poetry that grew out of a central line of Modernism—in Olson, and Creeley and Duncan and others—and it changed all the young writers in Canada as a result. Because the principle behind it is correct. It's the principle of authentic speech in relation to one's life and the particulars of existence. It's made for some lousy poetry, of course, but the principle itself is sound.[47]

Again, one sees how a poetry based on experience and authentic language can engage the particularist in Dudek without offending his rationalist side.

Dudek's essay on Souster, "Groundhog among the Stars," stands out as the only major essay which does not conform to Dudek's general theory of a "transition" in modern Canadian poetry from late-Victorian intellectual and emotional imprecision to a paradoxical combination of rationalism and realism.

As Warren Tallman has noted, Dudek curiously

forgets to bring his own previously articulated poetics to bear on Souster's work. Whether Souster has or hasn't moved in a functional prose realm of "thought itself" Dudek doesn't say. If the sounding of the poem fits in with Dudek's crucial insistence on "unique form" this too goes unmentioned. In fact, any of the means, music, methods by which Souster individualizes his attempts receives no attention whatsoever. Dudek's focus is exclusively on content without reference to forms. . . . [48]

In this essay Dudek seems to say that Souster is more important as an example of contemporary estrangement from reason and vision than as a guide to a new, authentic way of life. In "The Transition in Canadian Poetry," Dudek hailed Souster's anti-intellectualism as a valuable rejection of decadent nineteenth-century beliefs. Now Dudek again recommends Souster for his negative qualities: his grief, his boredom, his frustration, his fear of women. Dudek describes Souster as modern exemplary man, estranged from reason, trapped "in the modern urban situation," suffering "its private agonies"; because he is "involved in guilt in mankind, . . . Souster bears the fate of suffering with average mankind."[49] Dudek seems to imply that Souster is a perfect representative of modern experience, the very sort of person who needs the message of salvation contained in poems like Dudek's own *Europe* or *Atlantis*—that he is the average man whose estrangement from life and language "cultural custodians" like Arnold, Pound or Dudek labour to relieve.

In retrospect, it seems that Dudek's ability to accommodate paradox has been one very positive result of his dedication to reason. It has enabled him to hold profoundly contradictory opinions, to move simultaneously in different directions, in fact to move significantly towards that multiplicity of possibilities we know today as postmodernism. In his reaction against late Victorian literature, he could advocate that poetry be both "down-to-earth" and yet rich in "philosophical, contemplative content."[50] He could sympathize with the imagist call for "strong imagery, clarity of images, and also economy in the case of language in presenting the image"[51] yet also believe that the generally reductive push of the imagists and early modernists led to a "zero-point of negation" in both form and content which then demanded its own transcendence by poets working towards some "affirmation of larger life." In the early 1960s Dudek condemned much new writing for having "descended into a kind of slovenliness, shapelessness, and self-indulgence"[52] yet he himself tried to write "an infinite poem in progress," "a fragmentary and continuing process of meditation and creation" which "could document the real continual process of poetry-making that goes on inside the mind."

How much more interesting if we had T.S. Eliot's continual process of poetic thinking through the decades, not just the few poems that he thought he could polish up and finish![53]

Despite strong elitist and rationalist biases, Dudek also played a crucial part in the process whereby Canadian poetry turned away from modernist austerity and existentialist despair and towards the expansions and affirmations which characterize postmodernism. In a recent interview he guardedly admitted his role in this process.

After the seventeenth century began, it seems that each philosopher or writer has won his glory by taking something away; he was a greater writer because he revealed a more bitter and distasteful truth. So that's where I shifted, and I stopped teaching that business. I began to look in the other direction . . . what there is in the actual that is not mere nothingness and emptiness.[54]

Dudek is here referring to the essential shift from modernist to postmodernist aesthetics, from the aesthetics of economy to those of exuberant vision. This transition has been particularly important in Canada where modernism did not begin with the playfulness of Dada or the excesses of the primitivists, surrealists, constructivists or futurists, but with the technical austerities of early Joyce and Eliot. The shift to postmodernism does not lead Dudek to the adventurousness of Kroetsch, Coleman, Rothenberg or Mac Low, but it does lead him as early as the 1950s to open doors in that direction.

CHAPTER FIVE

Get the Poem Outdoors

I like to think I'm "talking out" my poems rather than consciously
dressing them up in the trappings of the academic tradition.

(Souster, dust jacket of *TEYS*)

Although Raymond Souster's formal statements about poetry
and poetics have been sporadic, brief and few, they have consistently expressed distaste for any potentially restricting
definition of poetry. In fact, Souster had more or less equated
such definitions with an attack on the vitality of the universe.
He held this extreme view as early as 1943 when he proposed
"Sperm" as the title for his first magazine (*Direction*). Souster
has usually associated poetry with "prolife" forces—with spontaneity, biological process, love and fertility; he classes those
who would bind poetry into inherited forms with the "antilife"
forces—with war, business, the academies and death. In de-
scribing his experience with "existing forms" in the preface to
Cerberus (1952), he spoke of "feeling bound within them,
mummified" (*C* 75). In 1965 he reacted to Cid Corman's assessment of *Ten Elephants on Yonge Street* by exclaiming, "I know I
get sloppy very often, too sentimental, but I *hope* I never get
Ezra Pound *cold*, Robert Creeley *controlled.* "[1]

This preference for a colloquial, spontaneous, undecorated poetry is in some respects an unsophisticated version of Dudek's "functional poetry" thesis. Like Dudek, Souster rejects cleverness in poetry, particularly the cleverness of the aestheticist who seeks consciously to dress his poetry in form for form's sake. Souster insists on the importance of intelligibility: "the primary function of poetry is to communicate something to somebody else" (*C* 75). He stresses the need for realism and credibility.

> Whomever I write to, I want to make the substance of the poem so immediate, so real, so clear, that the reader feels the same exhilaration — be it fear or joy — that I derived from the experience, object, or mood that triggered the poem in the first place.
>
> (Dust jacket of *TEYS*)

Souster shares Dudek's mistrust of literary criticism. He associates the critic with distortion, deliberate misreading and death.

> For his prying eyes dig
> into the darkest corners
> his ears pick up
> all sounds and distort them
> like disgruntled tuning forks.
>
> He is worse than Death
> and he is Everywhere.
>
> ("The Critic," *Y* 35)

However, Souster's theorizing lacks Dudek's clear sense of purpose and program. He rarely identifies the "opposition"; his literary antagonists are usually straw men similar to the unspecified bankers, bureaucrats, generals and politicians whom he condemns in many of his poems. He has only vague ideas about how his theories might be carried out in practice. Poetry is to be "exciting, germinative,"[2] "experimental and vigorous."[3] Most important, Souster lacks the large historical view of art and literature that Dudek has. Souster's pronouncements are ad hoc and intuitive opinions rather than reasoned, intellectual arguments.

Like the blind
leading the blind
      me here
at the end of the table
trying to tell all these young faces
about poetry
      when I don't know myself
which way to turn
which way to go

      ("7 St Nicholas," *ALP* 43)

Souster's most impressive aesthetic statement is the poem "Get the Poem Outdoors," which explicitly states his belief that poetry must be kindred to the "green world" of nature and to the spontaneous world of the common, unsophisticated person.

Get the poem outdoors under any pretext,	1
reach through the open window if you have to,	2
kidnap it right off the poet's desk,	3
then walk the poem in the garden, hold it up	4
among the soft yellow garlands of the willow,	5
command of it no further blackness, no silent	6
cursing at midnight, no puny whimpering	7
in the endless small hours, no more	8
shivering in the cold-storage room of the	9
winter heart,	10
tell it to sing again, loud and then louder so it	11
brings the whole neighbourhood out, but	12
who cares,	13
ask of it a more human face, a new tenderness,	14
even the sentimental allowed between the	15
hours of nine to five,	16
then let it go, stranger in a fresh green world, to	17
wander down the flower beds, let it go to	18
welcome each bird that lights on the still	19
barren mulberry tree.	20

      (*SFSG* [66])

This is not a statement of method. It tells very little about how a poem might be written, its syllables selected or its form discovered. Rather it is a general statement of conviction which is formally constructed so as to stand as its own illustration.

Fundamental to the poem is a conception of the natural world as joyful, open and creative. The true condition of this "outside" realm appears to be spring and summer; Souster does not consider the possibility of taking the poem "outside" into a winter landscape. Furthermore, "outside" is not barren pavement and roaring engines but a "garden" with "flower beds" and birds to "light" in the "mulberry tree." The poem should be part of a summer pastoral world, originating as close to nature as the poet's "open window" will permit. What goes on "outside" is of a higher order than what goes on "inside," and "outside" may trespass on "inside," as the instruction to "kidnap" reveals. The laws against intrusion, theft and kidnapping must defer to the higher laws of creativity and joy.

This idea that laws and conventions must be broken in order to create joy dominates the poem. The convention of the alienated, suffering poet (ll. 7–11), the convention that sentimentality in literature is undesirable (ll. 16–17) must all defer to the poem and its pursuit of " a more human face, a new tenderness." Although most of the terms here are vague (especially "a new tenderness"), the poem obviously proposes an iconoclastic role for poetry. Poetry is to upset both literary and social expectations; its standards are not to be those of literature and society but those of "outside," of songbird and flower border.

To be totally effective, a poem on aesthetics must live up to the standards which it proposes. "Get the Poem Outdoors" is a good piece of writing in this regard. Its form projects the same passionate, flexible "who cares" attitude that it identifies in nature. The trochaic imperatives "get," "reach," "kidnap" that begin the first three lines launch the poem with a rush of impatience. Once the poem is "outside," the tone relaxes slightly, and the imperatives become iambic ("then walk," "command"), even anapestic ("hold it up"), and the time gap between them increases. In lines 12 and following in which the tone relaxes even more, none of the imperatives receive primary stress; the emphasis, as Souster's ear correctly perceived, is no longer on the verb but on the environment, the "green

world" and the "mulberry tree." Other metrical subtleties contribute to the impressive way in which the poem remains "alive"
and changing throughout, like the "fresh green world" to which
it says all poems must aspire. In the second line the off-rhyme
of "window" with "have to" increases the line's speed. In lines 4
and 5 the half-rhyme of "garden" and "garlands" slows the lines
because of the delay in the rhyme and also because we are
surprised to find that "garlands" is not, like "garden," the
terminal word of its clause. Towards the end of the poem in
lines 15 and 17 the closely spaced rhyming phonemes of
"tenderness" and "sentimental" and of "allowed" and "hours"
create a sense of urgency and excitement leading up to the
climax. In the concluding lines the pace slows again due to the
interrupting appositive in line 18 and the repeated syntax of "let
it go to" in line 19.

Souster's strengths in this poem are those of the ear rather
than of the intellect. The denotative level of the poem is vague
and almost trite. For natural beauty it uses the commonplace
images of bird and flower. But through its technical qualities
the poem particularizes its own definition and illustrates what
kind of agile dance of syllables can occur when the poem is
truly "outside" convention and responsible only to its own
music.

The "outside" aesthetic of "Get the Poem Outdoors" is the
basis for many of Souster's most characteristic poems,
including those structured on a contrast between "inside" and
"outside" (between the urban and the rural, the manufactured
and the natural), those built around animal emblems and those
written to embody moments of whimsy. Because Souster's
aesthetic has not changed much since it first appeared in
Direction in 1943, the same kinds of poems can be found in every
period of Souster's writing. The inside/outside opposition is
evident in the opening poem of Souster's first book, *When We
Are Young* (1946). The first stanza of the poem presents a world
threatened by the "inside" forces of war and death, forces which
people are deliberately ignoring: "laughing too loudly to cover
up / the screech of guns, the stutter of death."

Until one day it was too late, one morning we woke and the
    blinds would not rise to salute the sun,
And the room was dark at noon, at six, at midnight when the
    clocks struck only once,

And we decided it must have been all a dream, a foolish, childish
    dream

That outside those windows birds had sung,
That up through green leaves we had seen the stars,
That we had worshipped life, that we had never thought of death.

                                    ("The Dragon," *WWAY* [3])

The two image clusters around "inside" and "outside" here are
strikingly similar to those of "Get the Poem Outdoors." "Inside"
is the world of habitual, self-deceiving action in which blind-
ness and lack of courage threaten the loss of "outside"; "outside"
is the sun, birds, green leaves, and life itself.

    The same dichotomy has been one of the main structural
elements in Souster's poetry throughout his career. The dichotomy accommodates a large number of themes: the poet's fear
of death, his hostility towards institutions, his mistrust of the
city and his fondness for those things which mitigate the negative effects of mortality, urbanization, big government and big
business — for love, nature, jazz, baseball and childhood. Fear
of death as an element of this structure takes two forms in *A
Local Pride* (1962). "Outside" terms — "sun," "boys," "trees,"
"flowers," "clouds" — dominate the first stanzas of "In Mount
Pleasant Cemetery."

> Impossible to think of death
> on such a pulsing afternoon.
>
> Sun catching changes of the leaves,
> boys flailing chestnut trees, the squirrels
> down and doing in the grass.
>
> Impossible to think of death,
> with flowers rioting on the slopes
> and cloud fleets sailing overhead.

The perceptual structure of the poem rests on a shift in the next stanza to "inside" imagery ("under all this ground the slow / rot and the patient worms work well") and on a concluding outside/inside paradox in which "to shout" is an "outside" action "impossible" for an enclosing tombstone.

> Even the tombstones seem to shout
> "Impossible, impossible."
>
> (*ALP* 82)

Another poem, "Twelve Mile Lake," also begins with "outside" imagery — references to childhood, trees, clouds.

> Mirror of childhood
> the water throws off
> swirl of the scrub pines
> puff of the clouds
> spill of the sun.

But here the "outside" imagery, enduring as one side of a paradox, is ultimately destroyed by its opposite.

> but look, like
> a cry for help
> echoed up from the rust
> of the rock-cool bottom,
>
> the eyes of a drowned girl.
>
> Smash this pretty mirror
> call these trees a lie
> clouds and sun a lie
>
> with my life the most perfect
> blackest lie of all.
>
> (*ALP* 85)

In Souster's poems about the inhumanity of governments, banks, churches and large businesses, this pessimistic version of the structure is dominant, particularly in poems where "death" is the ultimate result of the "inside" powers. In many of these poems the "outside" imagery is minimal, as in "No Escape" (*SFSG* 30) or "The End of the Day." These poems undoubtedly draw their "inside" imagery from Souster's years as a bank clerk.

> Now they hurry into elevators, and descend
> to streets where fresh air, traffic noise strike their faces,
> faces released for a few hours of play and sleep
> until alarm clocks jangle and the game resumes;
>
> leaving the stained fronts of banks, trusts, corporations,
> along with the lifeless air, dust settling silently
> on board-room furniture, in endless corridors,
>
> leaving behind like a poison gas the death smells
> of profit and loss, credits, margins,
> to hunt out the rats in their holes,
> kill them painlessly one by one.
>
> (*Y* 162)

In "The Pen and Ink Clerks" "outside" is reduced, after twenty-eight lines detailing the "failure," "disillusionment," and "fear" of the clerks and others victimized by "the slick ones," to an ironic cliché ("the good old days") in the concluding lines:

> Our pen and ink slides
> across our record books, our ledgers,
> and sometimes we imagine for a moment
> nothing has changed, that it's the same as before,
> as back in the good old days.
> No harm in that, dreams are still allowed.
>
> (*CU* [69])

This outside-cancelled-by-inside structure becomes the primary element in the epigrammatic "Very Short Poem":

> "... But only God can make a tree."
> (He'll never try it in Sudbury).
>
> (*SFSG* [89])

An interesting ambiguity enters Souster's inside/outside dichotomy in his poems about the city. The city's lights can be "golden lights / In diamond rows" ("The Hated City," *GTSW* 9) or "cold and mechanical" ("Lower Yonge Street," *GTSW* 12); the city's buildings can be "ghost buildings," "part of a tomb" ("Night Watch," *TSP* 38), "airless office tombs" ("A Letter from Mallorca," *L&F* 28), or "the dream palace / of my youth" ("Bingo Comes to the Runnymede," *CU* [87]). The ambiguity results from the fact that the city images have no fixed association with either of the core images of the dichotomy but instead change association according to context. Where the city is active in the destruction of "the dry black earth" ("Humber Valley Prospect," *TSP* III) and "red berries" ("Lambton Riding Woods," *CT* 16-17), its "apartments" and "ugly houses" are evil. Where its buildings shelter capitalist institutions ("Gasworks, Montreal East," *TSP* 98; "The End of the Day," *Y* 162) they are also evil. But where they shelter good food ("Night Watch," *TSP* 38), music ("Jazz Concert, Massey Hall," *TSP* 63), children ("The Tenement," *TEYS* 8) or love ("Dominion Square," *GTSW* 29), they join the "outside" imagery.

All of Souster's metaphors for love are derived from the cluster of "outside" images, and most of these come from nature. In "Dominion Square" the lovers "seem almost part of the rain / ... seem almost part of the night." Souster consistently speaks of the beloved in metaphors of trees, waterfalls and flowers:

> Trees after rain
> Lean against the wind.
> Clean limbs athletic,
> Are every inch delicate
> As young girls coming out of a pool,
> Who stand beautifully naked in the sun
> Shaking the water from their flanks
> Their shy awakening breasts.
>
> ("Trees after Rain," *GTSW* 56)

> Just in from the cold
> my hands touch your breasts

and your nipples shiver
like the petals of a flower
from which a butterfly
has just springboarded.
>> ("Just in from the Cold," *PM* 26)

From your slim waist to your thighs
curving like waterfalls, I read there
poems more wonderful than starlight. . . .
>> ("Shy One, Cautious One," *TEYS* 77)

In another instance Souster uses similar imagery for both himself and his beloved:

Why can't we be again
two awakened
shy green tree-buds
touched by the sun
opening toward each other?
>> ("Why Can't We Be Again," *ALP* 112)

However, Souster more frequently uses animal images for himself; in fact animals are the most common "outside" images in his poetry. Any animal found in Souster's Toronto habitat will do: skunks, cats, ducks, dogs, sparrows, spiders, canaries, caterpillars, fish, rabbits, cows, crows, starlings, wasps, bears, colts, bats, moths and groundhogs. In many cases Souster's appropriation of these creatures is subtle.

Caterpillar inching
up the sunward wall

I wish you tonight
same untroubled sleep

as my beloved
. . . . . .
caterpillar
of endearing patience
on the sunward wall.
>> "Caterpillar," *ALP* 81)

The animal need not become an explicit metaphor or emblem for Souster's personal condition. An anthropomorphic viewpoint allows him to project his own feelings directly onto the creature without necessarily acknowledging any conscious identification with it.

> The creek's dry,
> and the cattle that come here
> . . . .
> have piled the rock bed
> with their finest dung
> to show their disgust.
> ("The Farm out the Sydenham Road," *AI* 59)

Often the feelings projected into the animal are ones which Souster is apparently reticent to acknowledge—as in "Killing a Bat" where he evades a direct association by changing the pronoun in the last line from "you" to "they."

> You don't get rid
> of a bat by simply
> flushing him swiftly
> down the nearest toilet:
>
> he'll swoop and swerve
> through your head for days,
> . . . .
>
> who was perfectly content
> before being roused
> to rest on the curtains
> of this upstairs room.
>
> . . . .
> . . . his wings fight the air
>
> in a hopeless chance
> to escape, stay alive.
> But there's none, he dies,
> and they die a little too.
> (*L&F* 110)

At the other extreme are several poems in which Souster openly declares his identification with the anthropomorphized creature.

> . . . the spider's gauzy net
> clots my forehead, eyes,
>
> and I guess somewhere
> that spider curses me
> much as I curse him

(ALP 66)

Here the animal image acts primarily as a metaphor or emblem for the poet's condition. The poet is still projecting his feelings rather than directly expressing them, but with reference to the animal's situation rather than its anthropomorphized consciousness. These poems tend to be more credible than the others since the animal's situation is more grounded in fact than is an anthropomorphized animal consciousness.

Because "outside" is constantly threatened by "inside" in Souster's bipolar poetic consciousness, most of his animal emblems stand for the poet's own apprehensions about dangers in his environment. Most of these dangers involve death at the hands of "inside" forces. The fish lies "inside" the ground, not in a literal grave but in one of technology's gravelike excavations.

> Dead fish
> on the subway stairs
> eyes like no other
> I've ever seen
> . . . .
> already dead eyes
> have possessed and grow
> new eyes in me.

("Dead Fish," ALP 28)

The groundhog is about to succumb to a trap produced by a technology which has no sympathy for groundhogs, an "old lady lush," children, or poetry.

> The terrified look
> on the groundhog's face
> looking from his hole
> one instant ahead
> of the trap's deadly spring.
>
> I saw today
> in the ferret stare
> of the old lady lush
> up Bay Street somewhere,
> wandering like a child
>
> ("The Quarry," *ALP* 126)

In many cases the danger comes partly from the poet's own fear. This is indicated not by the victimization of the animal but by its heroism: the animal lives "with an earnestness, / a dedication to shame us humans" ("Wasp Nest," *AI* 69) and is often more active in defence of "outside" than the poet himself.

> Old buzzard crow cawing his head off
> in one of our three ragged fir trees.
>
> Trying to make later April
> out of early March
> . . . .
> out of winter death.
>
> Death I tell him,
> that's all I feel right now.
>
> but try again next month;
> don't give up on the world
> and most of all on me.
>
> ("Old Buzzard Crow," *CU* [101])

Given Souster's usual equation of love with natural processes and "outside" imagery, one would expect him to use the same images for sexuality. But he does not. In fact, in Souster's early poems sexuality is often classed with the "inside" forces. It is specifically linked to death and commerce.

A dime will slap a hamburger between your teeth,
For two bits the usual stretch in a movie heaven,
And a dollar unlocks the dark door of sex.

("The Payoff," *WWAY* [22])

Sex is either unsatisfying ("Ersatz," *WWAY* [27]) or it casts the lover into the equivocal role of nature's "delighted" murderer.

My fingers reach down
Into the dew-wet hairs of the grass
And tighten around your
Slender arms, . . .
. . . I have to sever those
Arms from the earth, and each time
I feel like a murderer, delighting
In another orgy of killing
Something that breathes and has life more
Beautiful, more wonderful than my own.

("Violets," *GTSW* 41)

Souster's ambivalence about human sexuality and the human body is less obvious in his later work where he uses metaphor (see "Migration," *AI* 54; "God-like," *SFSG* [24]) or an impersonal viewpoint (see "Homecoming," *CT* 100) to avoid any direct contemplation of the subject. However, it is still apparent in poems like "The Embarrassment" in which Souster feels disturbed in the presence of a woman friend who is publicly breast-feeding her baby:

So that I mutter
words, any words,
so that I want so desperately to drop
the rye, the ginger ale,
to back out, to hide,
anything but raise my eyes. . . .
And I repeat—this thing you do
the most natural thing in the world.

(*L&F* 102)

In the much anthologized "The Hunter," Souster communicates this same ambivalence through an animal emblem. Here the animal, a groundhog, is already dead, killed by a young woman with whom the narrator appears to have some involvement. The sexual attractiveness of the young woman is linked to the "inside" elements of death, traps, guns and the technology that produces them. The narrator connects his own "fate" to that of the "outside" forces, to the slain groundhog, to the "imaginary rabbits" being shot at by "the half-wit hired man." Despite the obvious fascination with death, sexuality and violence that the poem reveals, the effect of the image structure is to place imagination and sexuality in opposing camps.

> . . . I watch the swing of your girl's hips
>   in the cotton dress
> Ahead of me, the proud way your hand carries the gun, and
>   remembering how you held it
> Up to the hog caught in the trap and blew his head in,
> Wonder what fate you have in store for me.
>
> (*WWAY* [5])

Most of Souster's poetry has embedded in its structure an ambivalence about inside/outside that parallels this ambivalence about sexuality. Despite the thematic assertions of allegiance to "outside," most of the poetry displays a man who observes the "outside" without directly participating in it ("The Embarrassment," "Old Buzzard Crow," "The Quarry," "Caterpillar"), who observes "outside" from "inside"—from inside a bank or a suburban house, and often from within a detached consciousness.

> Lightning's
> wildest flash
> tamed to
> flame-flutter
>
> fires today
> the murmurous
> green of my
> poplar tree
>
> ("The First Scarlet Tanager," *AI* 96)

Cool, detached "inside" language often coexists with engaged colloquiality: "how you held it / up to the hog caught in the trap and blew his head in." Images which Souster has made "inside" and conventional to his poetry—birds, trees, clouds and love vs. commerce, war, pavement and death—are presented in the language of "outside"—in natural speech rhythms and in realistic diction. Seldom, however, does Souster wholly commit himself to being an "outside" person; instead he usually withdraws, as we shall see in the next chapter, into predictable imagery, distancing wit and the epigrammatic last line (as in "The Hunter") which abruptly precludes any further exploration of the experience.

The exceptions to this inside/outside ambivalence are Souster's wry or whimsical poems, like "Get the Poem Outdoors" in which the poet is clearly going beyond the bounds of expectation, convention and reason in terms of form as well as of expressed idea. Here Souster fully participates in the "outside" process, becoming joyous, imaginative, reckless, wasteful and irreverent. He also abandons his usual images and emblems, or else deals with them in an unexpected way. Animals are anthropomorphized, but into amusing absurdity—as in the case of Charlie the spider who is perplexed to find a rose petal trapped in his web.

> What to do? Charlie didn't like
> the taste of it, the thing took up
> far too much trapping area,
> and yet gave the place a little class
> . . . .
> Then one day, inspiration!
> He painted up a sign in bug's blood,
> hung it out proudly:
>
> HAPPY CHARLIE'S ROSE GARDENS
> WHERE YOU'LL ALWAYS MEET A FRIEND
> ("The Spider Outside Our Window," *CU* [28])

Other nature images are also made to display an amusing and unpredictable energy that directly upsets "inside" expectation and stability. A rainbow defies a mayor and "his councillors" and sucks "up half of Lake Simcoe" and drops it "softly in Lake Couchiching" ("Rainbow Over Lake Simcoe," *CT* 108); the Niagara River aids Canadian literature by sweeping "twenty minor poets over the Horseshoe Falls" ("The Goat Island Poetry Conference," *CT* 64).

In these whimsical poems, the imagination triumphs thematically through the victory of "outside" over "inside" and aesthetically through the way in which Souster breaks up the expected elements in his writing. The realistically portrayed destitute/cripple figure so common in Souster's poetry becomes in the following remarkable poem a surreal representative of all humanity and its irrational appetites; the language here also achieves a far more economical and suggestive texture than usual. Souster's need to make an explicit point, which so often dominates his poems, is entirely overcome; the poem approaches the subtlety and indirection of drama.

Seeing the wedding was off I had no good use for the wedding cake. Spying the local idiot, I printed on a huge placard the block letters of EAT and pushed the cake at him. He at once began pulling it down over his head as if it were a hat. So I grabbed it back from him and held up the placard again. This time he seemed to get the right idea, but he put the whole damn cake in his mouth and began to choke.

Even then I couldn't get mad at him. After all, he didn't have any more real use for that cake than I had.

("Silly Little Poem," *SFSG* [37])

In the whimsical poems, sexual desires no longer generate Souster's conventional imagery of birds and trees, but rather move characters to absurd yet poetically "true" actions and lead the poet to an admirable deftness of technique. In "The Mating Season" a husband, at his wife's half-joking suggestion, cuts off his legs because their "lack of suppleness" has given "trouble lovemaking." Like the wife's suggestion, the tone of the poem is "half-joking":

Now in bed
when he inches over with his stumps

> she turns her back on him. Ugh,
> she murmurs
>
> to think that I
> with all my beauty
> should have ended up marrying a cripple!
>
> (*Y* 102)

Again this poem uses the indirect method of drama, so that all the complexities of sexual desperation and tragedy are merely implied by the situation.

The most memorable images and metaphors in Souster's poetry are virtually confined to his whimsical poems. These images — jazz, baseball, the roller coaster, the rocket ship, the high-speed elevator — all show the imagination in the process of triumphing over death, commerce, bureaucracy, boredom, the law and other incarnations of "inside" ideology: "When Rocky Nelson shuffles up to the plate / ... / He takes up his stance which ignores every law" ("The Ballad of Rocky Nelson," *PM* 28). Art and imagination succeed by defeating expectation and tradition.

> ... the runner going into second
> Took one quick look at that boat
> And yelled, Hey look, they got
> My old lady's black pants
> Flying there at the masthead!
> . . . .
> And went in to score standing up.
>
> ("The Opener," *TSP* 88)

Thus the poet who designs and builds a "monster space rocket" in "The Launching" uses it unexpectedly to entrap "cabinet ministers, generals, munitions makers," and calls these men "the boys on the inside."

The informing concept of "The Launching" is the surprising nature of art. Again, both the reader and the law are taken by surprise as the poem matter-of-factly unfolds.

> When the Big Day came
> they stood on a platform at the foot of the monster

and made speeches one after another.
I let them talk as long as they wanted to,
then when the last one had finished
I pushed back a little door
in the side of my brain child
and invited them to enter.

When the last one had disappeared inside
I closed the door, walked very deliberately
across to the control panel
and pushed a button.
                    It worked.

                                        (*ALP* 124)

A careful reading of this poem reveals how accurately its language embodies the inside/outside antithesis. The calm and mocking narrative voice is clearly that of the "outside" skeptically deriding the "inside." By capitalizing "Ceremony of the Officials" and "Big Day" the poet ridicules the false sense of importance which officialdom gives to its own activities. The narrator, on the other hand, uses the terminology of the "little man" who minimizes the importance of his own creations. Despite having built a rocket he has absorbed none of the pretensions of scientific and technical language; his rocket is his "brain child," its hatch "a little door." The difference between this man, to whom all wasted words are pretension, and the garrulous officials whom he lets "talk as long as they wanted to" is brilliantly conveyed by the laconic last line: "It worked."

Souster's most extensive venture into the "outside" poem is "The Flight of the Roller-Coaster." Unlike the "monster space rocket," this flight of imagination does not carry "insiders" but rather some anonymous riders and a "cucumber-cool / Brakeman." The tone of this poem is also matter-of-fact, and implies that the fantastic should be, if not commonplace, at least not an unusual part of our world. Once again Souster's inside/outside dichotomy pervades: the roller coaster is a "movieland magic carpet, some wonderful bird"; it triumphs over the conventional world where "amusement" is confined to the "amusement park."

... without fuss or fanfare [it] swooped slowly across the
                amusement park,
Over Spook's Castle, ice-cream booths, shooting gallery;
                and losing no height

Made the last yards above the beach where the cucumber-cool
Brakeman in the last seat saluted
A lady about to change from her bathing-suit.

Then, as many witnesses duly reported, headed leisurely
                over the water....

                           (*TSP* 132)

    As in "Get the Poem Outdoors," the quality of Souster's writing here is equal to the aesthetic values which the poem implies. Like the roller coaster, the baseball player or the jazz musician, Souster "improvises" his way through his chosen structure and medium. When the roller coaster takes flight, his words do also, keying on the word "swoop" to launch a series of accented $[u]$ syllables: "Spook's," "booths," "shooting," "losing," "cucumber-cool," "saluted." Short parallel phrases speed the roller coaster on its way "over Spook's Castle, ice-cream booths, shooting galleries" and modulate into longer rhythmic phrases when the vehicle levels from its "swoop" into a fixed course across the lake. With the "swoop" concluded, the dominant vowel sound gradually shifts from $[u]$ to the longer $[e]$: "Made," "Brakeman," "lady," "change," "bathing." This pattern ends abruptly when the concluding lines shift attention from the roller coaster to the reactions of onlookers. There is no dominant vowel in these lines but instead a very large number of liquid consonants — $[l]$, $[r]$, $[w]$ — which contribute greatly to the peaceful and satisfied mood in which the poem ends.

    "Flight of the Roller-Coaster" represents Souster at the height of his talents, able to improvise with language in a manner equal to the improvisational abilities of his "outside" masters in baseball and jazz. The poem is a model of organic form, of what Dudek calls "the music ... of your sounds as they fit the content of your poetry." And yet the most fascinating aspect of the poem is not its form at all. It is the fact that

Souster—unlike Chaucer with his eagle, or Keats "on the viewless wings of Poesy"—is not aboard his winged fantasy but remains on the ground quietly lamenting its disappearance "all too soon behind a low-lying flight of clouds."

CHAPTER SIX

The Penny Flute

He was not playing
For an audience, but almost for himself.

(Souster, "The Penny Flute," *TSP* 18)

In the preceding chapter we saw how the major image clusters in Souster's work have their source in the same concerns as do his diction and his explicit aesthetic statements. The inside/ outside dichotomy is organic to every aspect of Souster's work — his conscious beliefs about poetry, his habitual imagery and his deepest feelings about personal, social and political relationships.

This is not the usual approach to Souster's poetry. Most critics, including Dudek in "Groundhog among the Stars," have offered more thoroughly thematic explanations of their attraction to his writing. They have commented that Souster's "themes are love, death and loneliness, ... some of his best poems are crammed with local landmarks."[1] They have pointed out "the themes of a family past, now lost, set against a barren and violent present with a few brief pleasures."[2] Or, like Gary Geddes, they have focussed on how Souster's poetry is "rooted" in Toronto and

crammed with that city's beggars, pimps, cripples, prostitutes, news-

boys, ball players, and architectural landmarks; they...
move ... speaking of a city which, though it changes its cosmetic
hourly, is still recognizable. [3]

Personally, I have strong reservations about the usefulness
of such criticism. While it does identify certain ideas and concerns in Souster's work with which almost any humane person
of this century can sympathize, it does not say much to explain
the specific appeal of the writing. As Warren Tallman has remarked about this type of criticism, it reveals "nothing one
might not have guessed of almost any sensitive modern poet
without reference to his poems." [4]

A more useful way of coming to terms with the "social"
aspects of Souster's poetry would be to examine more closely
the aesthetic relationship between his language and his
philosophical concerns. Much of Souster's writing will respond
to being read in openly Marxist terms. His choice of diction,
subjects, stanza forms and syntax can be viewed as political
choices, even as political gestures. It is easy to overlook this
feature of Souster's writing because of the nonphilosophical and
nonintellectual character of both the man and his poetry. Yet
there are definite political overtones in the very fact that
Souster tries to avoid the role of expert or authority. This,
together with the explicit anticapitalist sentiments expressed in
such poems as "The Launching" (*SP* 60), "The Pen and Ink
Clerks" (*CU* [69]), "The End of the Day" (*Y* 162) and "First
Spring Day in Canyons" (*TSP* 123), gives additional significance to those qualities in Souster's imagery, syntax and diction which have been variously described as "the language of
common speech," [5] "crisp images," "peculiar narrowness," [6]
"ordinariness," [7] "the shifting rhythms of speech." [8] Critics have
been puzzled by these qualities, which confront them with the
awkward paradox of a "common" or "ordinary" style which
nevertheless has an extraordinary effect. This paradox has led
the anthologists Geddes and Bruce to suggest both that Souster
is "predominantly a poet of content" and that "his best poems
are either pure image or pure voice." [9] In an attempt to explain
the paradox, Robert Fulford has written,

we may succumb to the notion that Souster's poetry is as ordinary as his lifestyle, that these bits of observation are as commonplace as a bank teller's handwriting. But they aren't.

Souster's poems, however often they are rooted in the ordinary data of everyday life, concern the eternal subjects of poetry: love, beauty, hatred, above all death. Furthermore, they are as carefully carved, as firmly and maturely conveyed, as anything in Canadian poetry in this period. [10]

But exactly how Souster's poems are "carefully carved," neither Fulford nor Geddes and Bruce, who call the poems "beautifully turned," have been able to explain.

A Marxist approach to literary form [11] might help resolve the puzzle. According to Marxist theory, there is a division in bourgeois literature between creator and consumer which parallels a similar division between producer and consumer in bourgeois economic life. This division, which developed sometime during or before the sixteenth century, destroyed the sense of literature as a social creation and substituted the idea that a literary work is the product of an individual author who is removed from his audience both by physical circumstance and by the machinery of publishing. One effect of this division is to establish separate roles for author and reader. Author and reader become like transmitter and receiver, with a one-way relationship similar to McLuhan's description of the relationship between the "hot" print or film media and a passive audience. A second effect of this division is the elevation of "content," whether ethical, instructional, practical or recreational. The text possesses value to the consumer, as do other purchases, through its utility. So that in the current decade Margaret Atwood's guide to Canadian literature, *Survival*, has more readers than her novel *Surfacing*, Arthur Hailey's *Airport* more than *Survival*, and various "how-to-do-it" manuals more than both criticism and fiction together. Linguistic and literary signs are no longer either autotelic or identical with their significations, but instead they become referential and gain utility by their connection to realities outside the text. "What's it about?" becomes the most significant literary question. The literary work is thus effectively transformed, as Louis Dudek feared, into a commodity. The poem and its offspring, the novel and literary criticism, become objects to be sold and bought in a marketplace, the products of a commercial publishing process that involves a division of labour between editors, typesetters, designers, pressmen, binders, distributors and retailers. This process even creates its own "consumer reports" in the form of book reviews written by intermediaries between author and reader whose role is to certify the value of the product.

Writers become commodities, too. They are exhibited at publishing parties, book signings, poetry readings. Their celebrity status adds to the value of their books and creates a consumer demand that publishers must satisfy by urging writers to produce more. Louis Dudek, who opposed the commercialization of literature on elitist rather than Marxist principles, observed that a number of Canadian poets, including Cohen, Layton and Purdy, were openly inviting a popular response to their work.

Cohen, Layton, Purdy — to rank them by their rating — are all three generous exploiters of sex as an entertainment come-on, very much like the skin movies and advertisements that play for gross audience response. They're the Belly Dancers of poetry, with Layton as the star attraction. [12]

To Dudek, who had deliberately prevented his own work from becoming an aesthetic commodity, these poets were involved in "an error that none of the great moderns could conceivably have tolerated." [13]

The struggle against the commercialization of literature, against the transformation of art into applied art, was, as Dudek suggests, a central effort of the early modernists. It is present in the Dada resistance to content, in the surrealists' radical view of consciousness and in the imagists' objections to description. It is a declared theme in Pound's *Hugh Selwyn Mauberley*, particularly in its portrait of Arnold Bennett ("Mr. Nixon"), and an implicit one in Eliot's depiction of a culture transformed by its Smyrna merchants into a wasteland of "marketplace" sex and literature.

Souster's personal precedents in early Anglo-American modernism are the closely related movements of minimalism and imagism. Souster seems to have been influenced by minimalism through his close friend W.W.E. Ross and Ross's fascination with haiku and by imagism through William Carlos Williams. Minimalism resists directly the quantitative emphases of commodity fetishism. In a culture based on giantism, on continuing increases in industrial production, in standards of living, in the scale of aircraft and buildings, minimalism announces the contrary doctrine that "less is more." Minimalism declares that the inconspicuous, the unpretentious, the simple, have more innate power than their inflated, decorated, extended or complicated counterparts.

Souster's use of minimalist principles begins at the level of subject matter. What appears to be a thematic interest in what Geddes and Bruce list as "whores, cripples, beggars, down-and-outs of every sort" [14] is equally an aesthetic decision about the location of artistic power. Souster writes about the condition of being dwarfed, and by this act he asserts the "less is more" paradox that more significance resides in dwarfdom than in the inflated commodity structures which loom above. In "Night Watch," the large — the industrial city's buildings — is deathly, but the small is dogged and alive.

> Here under ghost buildings, here with silence
> grown too silent;
> You and I in the doorway like part of a tomb,
> Kissing the night with bitter cigarettes.
>
> (*TSP* 38)

In "The Penny Flute," the contrast is again between the small — an old man and his penny flute — and the Brobdingnagian images of commodity production.

> An old man . . . playing a penny flute.
> The sound was small and sweet, almost a

> whisper against the muffled roar
> Of the machinery of the cloth factory across the
> street.

Souster distinguishes between the factory and the old man, who is not engaged in producing goods for consumption: "He was not playing / For an audience, but almost for himself" (*TSP* 18).

The metaphysical relationship between large and small is stated clearly by Souster in another early poem, "Sunday Night Walk." Here a young couple detach themselves from the city crowds whose entrapment in the consumption circuit is indicated by the "restaurants" allusion.

> ... crowds
> Careless and gay tonight though there is nothing
> For them to do but walk and rewalk these streets
> Or crowd the corner hamburgers, restaurants.

The couple leaves this scene for a park which Souster declares

> ... is real grass, it is green, the pond at the bottom
> Of the road is a real pond and the real moon in it,
> Even the two ducks floating upon it are real,
>
> And we are real, our love is real,
> the world real, very real

Yet paradoxically this "world" is also, as the street scene indicated, reluctant to acknowledge these humble sources of its true meaning.

> But the world is tired, very tired of reality.
>
> (*TSP* 31)

A list of "small" subject matter affirmed as "real" in Souster's poetry would be nearly as long as a list of his published poems. The world of "small" things includes animals, insects, trees, flowers, lovers, baseball players, jazz musicians, anonymous World War II fliers ("Death of the Dawn Patrol,"

TSP 65), old ladies ("Breakfast: Old Lady in Hospital," *TSP* 113; "Death by Streetcar," *TSP* 129; "The Ugliest Woman," *TSP* 127; "Hospital Corridor," *EI* 159) and lost young women ("Girl with the Face of Sores," *TSP* 87; "Jeannette," *TSP* 89; "The Negro Girl," *TSP* 122; "Girl at the Corner of Elizabeth and Dundas," *TSP* 128), as well as the "cripples, beggars, down-and-outs" his reviewers have publicized. Usually these subjects have been victimized by the larger "cement" forms of contemporary culture.

> I should pull out this stubborn little bush
> growing out half between the brick
> of the house and the driveway's cement.
>
> ("Little Bush," *EI* 135)

This faith in the value of the minimal closely resembles Dudek's belief in the poetic power of the uninspired moment or trivial reflection. By focussing on the rejected, the humble, the easily overlooked, Souster implies not only that these elements of society deserve our attention but that they possess a strength and greatness in direct proportion to the commodity culture's neglect of them.

Related to this choice of subject matter is Souster's choice of casual observations as the occasions of his poems. The force of such a choice — again similar to Dudek's choice of subject in *Atlantis* — is to argue ontological importance for the temporally limited reflection or experience.

> At the end of the eavestrough
> winter's first icicle
> now pierced by the sun
> and dying
> one stubborn drop at a time.
>
> ("Now in November," *CU* [73])

Here the "trivial" subject, an icicle, is observed casually and briefly, and its fate is both invested with irony through the unexpected transference of the "pierced" image and linked to the reader's fate through the anthropomorphic functioning of "stubborn." Through this reference to the reader, the poet indirectly states that the reader too is significant and, by further implication, that the reader's perceptions are also worth attention.

This exemplary quality of Souster's perceptions is more readily experienced than recognized intellectually. Souster usually achieves the effect, much like Dudek in *Europe* and *En México*, by launching directly into a perceptual experience so that the reader becomes immediately involved in the process of recognition.

> A bird with a berry
> big as its head tries
> to carry it across
> the back grass, gets half way
> then drops it.

This technique creates the illusion that the reader's and the writer's experiences are simultaneous and that the images are common property; overall there is a blurring of the distinction between the act of writing and the act of reading.

Often Souster follows this technique, as in "The Response" (*EI* 65), "The Embarrassment" (*L&F* 102) and the above poem, with a dramatic presentation of his own response to the perceptual material. The reader, who is already identifying with the writer perceptually, is then caught up into the activity of the response.

> When I asked him
> why he doesn't pick it up again
> he answers, "I'm just not
> in the mood . . .

Again the line between reader and writer is obscured. The poet never tells the reader directly how to respond. In the conclusion to this particular poem, he obscures another distinction (between animals and humans) and declines to provide any final explanation.

which only proves birds
are no better than humans
at answering questions.

("Bird with a Berry," *EI* 127)

At the level of language, Souster's poems do not resemble
aesthetic commodities because he avoids — again very much
like Dudek — all semblance of a carefully machined or manufactured surface. As John Sutherland remarked of Souster's
earliest work, "Mr. Souster has . . . tried to look as little like a
poet as he could . . . he writes in a plain unvarnished manner
that avoids all but the simplest technique as literary
affectation." [15] Souster's language is visibly nonliterary and
appears selected with minimal care. The tone is casual, impulsive, colloquial. Syntax is still directive; that is, the reader is
not allowed to create the syntactical relationships among the
items of the poem's vocabulary (as later poets such as
McCaffery and Bissett have allowed). But the syntax is often
compressed or elided,

Not dead drunk
or he wouldn't be writhing like that
half up half down

("Lombard St., One PM," *EI* 96)

or confused by apparent "errors" in modification,

But my shame
coming on you in the kitchen,
unprepared for the great hanging tit,
the suckling infant,

("The Embarrassment," *L&F* 102)

so that the usual authority of the text is subverted and its effect
is more dramatic than directive. This quality invests nearly all
of Souster's poems with the indirectness of dramatic mono-
logue.

In Souster's declared dramatic monologues substandard

diction and exclamatory, telescoped syntax create poems that are nearly pure oral image rather than verbal direction.

> You want it or you don't
> You got five bucks or no
> I'm twenty-one I ain't
> Got any time to waste
> You want it or you don't
> Make up your jesus mind
>
> ("Girl at the Corner of Elizabeth and Dundas," *TSP* 128)

The economy of language here is another example of the minimalist impulse in Souster and also an indication of his attachment to imagism, itself a variant of minimalism.

The most celebrated examples of imagism in Souster's poetry are "The Six Quart Basket" and "Study: The Bath." In both theme and form "The Six Quart Basket" lies outside the commodity exchange processes of contemporary culture. The six-quart basket was once a part of these processes, containing fruits or vegetables on their journey from producer to consumer. It is now useless, "one side gone / half the handle torn off." The poem's form is nondirective — a series of concrete perceptions unmodified by value judgements or authorial interpretation. Of the three adjectives in the poem, two indicate quantity ("*six quart* basket", "*one* side") and the third colour ("*white* fruits"). The extreme austerity of the language echoes both the spareness of the ruined basket and the simplicity of its burden — "the white fruits of the snow" — neither of which has commodity value. The basket is affirmed, however, as "central," with the word "centre" lying in the exact syllabic centre of the fourth line.

> sits in the centre of the lawn
>
> (*ALP* 130)

The basket's new cargo is not mere snow; it is "the white fruits of the snow." The image suggests a fruitfulness in nature beyond the material utilities of purchase and sale.

"Study: The Bath" confronts the familiar issue of language

as commodity as well as a new issue, the role of women as sexual commodities. In terms of language, the Marxist avoidance of description, didactic content or the commodity fetishism of the aesthetic object is as clear as anywhere in Souster's work. Again the language is nondirective, free of interpretative modifiers; the diction ("buttocks," "crotch") jabs at literary decorum; the images are presented directly and in the sequence of someone perceiving rather than ordering: a dimly lit bathroom, a woman stepping from the tub, her body, its slightness, the reader's eyes moving like "the glistening water" down the woman's body to "the slightly plumed / oval of crotch." The result is that the reader becomes the perceiver, almost the author of the poem, receiving the images and forming content and meaning out of the raw data.

The central image of a naked young woman emerging from a bathtub has resonances in numerous directions: nineteenth-century paintings of bathers and reclining nudes, photo spreads in men's magazines, TV commercials for soaps and shampoos. The voyeuristic overtones of all these resonances are present here in the opening perspective. Reader and author gaze into the "almost dim light" ("*almost* dim," but only dim enough to make one look more keenly, not enough to impede one's view) of a bathroom where the naked woman is quietly unaware of their presence.

> In the almost dim light
> of the bathroom a woman
> steps from the white tub
> towel around her shoulders.

In the second stanza the suggestion of an idealized woman, woman as sexual commodity, lurks in much of the diction ("glisten," "slight," "tight belly," "slightly plumed") but the idealization is simultaneously held in check, almost criticized, by the more factual diction which interrupts and concludes the image ("buttocks," "crotch").

In the third and fourth stanzas, the perspective changes from that of a viewer to that of the woman herself—to "her

attention." The "sex-object" imagery is replaced by the image of
a woman who treats her body as her own organic possession.
The idealizing diction of the second stanza also vanishes, and
the poem settles, as it did at the end of the second stanza, on
the woman's factual humanity.

> eyes collected
> her attention gathered
> at the ends of fingers
>
> as she removes
> dead skin from her nipples.
>
> *(TSP* 82)

The implied antagonism here to the transformation of
reality into a commodity object is a common element in
Souster's work. One finds it in "Humber Valley Prospect"
where "young not-yet-ripened carrots / out of the dry black
earth" have been transformed into apartment buildings.

> But the farm's gone, field's gone, whole valley
> Flattened out, grass-stripped, a thing
> Neither for praise nor beauty. And these rows
> Of apartment blocks with only the ugliness
> Showing. . . .
>
> *(TSP* III)

Souster makes the same point ironically in "Beggar in the
Subway," which begins with the beggar "holding out pencils for
you to buy" but quickly moves into a description of the beggar
himself as the actual object for sale.

> But much more than that
> he offers you, absolutely free of charge,
> his equally yellowed face, his eyes that hold
> only darkness, that look and do not look
> at you, he'll throw in even
> the stumps of his legs and his crutches
>
> *(CU* [39])

Several of Souster's poems, like "The Twenty-fifth of December," attack the commercialization of Christmas,

> Hark the herald angels sing
> All sales final
> Peace on earth and mercy
> To all cash customers

> (*TSP* 53)

and others deplore commercialization of poetry. "Light and Shadow," for instance, accuses James Reaney of writing poetry which is deliberately decorated and inflated in order to make a better impression in the literary marketplace. Souster's criticism of Reaney is strongly reminiscent of Dudek's remarks in *Europe* about the "smoothies" of the seventeenth century who turned architecture into a commodity ("the smoothies . . . cut an arch or a cornice / with the brainless exactitude / of precision instruments / and made them all alike" *E* [69]).

> Casa Loma lights blazing,
> Cars glide up, unloading
> The dancers of the evening . . .

> (Go to it, Jim Reaney
> You finish it off with witches brewing
> a cauldron for the CAA
> In the centre of the Great Hall

These opening stanzas tie Reaney, rather arbitrarily, to various architectural and artistic excesses — to the ostentatious late-Edwardian mansion Casa Loma of Sir Henry Pellatt, to the self-promotions of the Canadian Authors' Association and to the rather exhibitionistic mock-heroic narratives (specifically *The Witches' Brew*) of E.J. Pratt. In the following stanzas Souster proceeds past Casa Loma to a "private nursing home" where a friend lies gravely ill,

> Waiting for the goddam nurse
> To come with some dope

> And relax the hands
> Of . . . beautiful pain.

At the poem's conclusion he turns sarcastically back to Reaney, accusing him now of not only writing poems which ignore and conceal the extravagances of the wealthy, but of falsely beautifying human suffering.

> (Go to it, Jim Reaney
> You finish it maybe
> With a laughing fanciful
> Sally at the moon).

> > (*TSP* 52)

In its cryptic and unfinished evocation of the sick friend, and in its sketchy and allusive attack on Reaney, "Light and Shadow" is an expression of sardonic minimalism. It isolates the act of saying too much — architecturally through Casa Loma or verbally through the "fanciful sally at the moon" — and shows how this kind of overstatement paradoxically fails to say enough about the realities of death and suffering. Souster's poem embodies the directness of word and image which it recommends and, like "Bird with a Berry," involves the reader in the creation of the poem by presenting only dramatic and visual images that are — to borrow a term from Lévi-Strauss — "uncooked" by authorial interpretation.

Souster's resistance to the commodity culture extended beyond his writing to his publishing ventures and his presentation of himself as an artist. His magazines *Direction, Enterprise, Combustion* and *Contact* were all crudely produced, with no attempt to lure readers through packaging or typography. Most of the Contact Press books he produced were mimeographed, and even the celebrated *New Wave Canada* anthology was offset onto newsprint from typed copy and bound in a black and white cover. Souster has also "discouraged" the growth of his personal reputation, in Dudek's words, by his "unwillingness to play the personality game and to go on tours and readings." [16] This reluctance has probably prevented Souster from acquiring the kind of public persona which has helped to popularize the work of writers of similar stature, such as Birney, Purdy and Atwood.

Suspicion of the commodity values of their culture was a primary tie between Souster and Dudek — a tie which transcended their intellectual and temperamental differences. It united them in their early publishing ventures and provided the one major thematic link between their work. Both men rejected programmatic Marxism. Souster adopted an automatic suspicion of authority and pretension whether in art or literature; Dudek often attempted, like Arnold and Carlyle, to counter the spurious authority of "barbarian" commercialism with his personal authority as a cultural commentator. In so doing, he adopted the producer/consumer, teacher/student model. Yet at other times, as we have seen, he qualified his authority by presenting his ideas, as in *Europe* and *En México*, dramatically and without intellectual framework. In these instances, the poet drops his role as teacher, and becomes, like Souster, an exemplary figure with whom the reader can identify. Dudek's work rarely shows the influence of Marxist antagonism to overt thematic content as Souster's best work does. Dudek never considered explicit content a source of weakness in literature; on the contrary, he believed that the transformation of content-bearing literature into an aesthetic object lessened its inherent effectiveness, as in the case of Pound's *Cantos*. Nevertheless, despite their differences, Dudek and Souster both vigorously opposed the commercialization of art and humanity in their culture and the dishonesty, decorativeness, self-promotion, and publicity seeking that accompanied it. Souster would unquestionably accept Dudek's rather bitter epigram:

Contemporary fame is like sugar, a pure white poison.

(*Ep* 32)

CHAPTER SEVEN

A Long-Lost World

You never get under enough for me, you always seem to stop short of entering the subject approached, always seem to be satisfied with a somewhat sentimental response that suggests a warm social conscience and yet somewhat hazy, if not lazy. [1]

This was Cid Corman's assessment of Souster shortly after having received from him the collection *For What Time Slays* (1955). Corman's "always" here is apparently hyperbolic; he admired "Flight of the Roller-Coaster," first published in *For What Time Slays*, and in a letter of 30 April 1964 termed it a "perfect" poem. [2] Yet he continued to stand by the essence of his criticism: that there are numerous Souster poems which achieve much less than they promise because they move directly from an idiosyncratic perception into habitual responses and into habitual imagery and language. This is a criticism to which Souster himself made little objection and which is often sustained by an examination of the poetry.

In some of his poems Souster seems to resort to literary conventions or social pieties in order to evade the radical implications of his images or insights. The earliest sign of this evasiveness is Souster's weakness for rhetorical structure; almost one-half of the poems in *Go to Sleep, World* (1947) rely on repeated parallel clauses.

Not in the noonday crowds,
Not a waking,
Not with the hard warm sunlight
In the park, . . .

No, it is not then,

It is when the sun is gone, when the lights are in the streets,
When the people walk those streets, when the couples. . . .

("When Night Comes," *GTSW* 2)

This use of rhetoric, which implies a postured rather than a responsive attitude towards his subject, occurs in Souster's work throughout his career.

Nobody argues that his chest wasn't crushed,
nobody argues that he died without a cry,
nobody argues that he died without any time for pain.

Not time either for any vice-president of the corporation
to express a vote of thanks on behalf of the management,
no time either for . . .
no time either for . . .
no time for anything . . .
no time so. . . .

Only time to. . . .

("Death on the Construction Site," *Y* 22)

This rhetorical mode is the anitithesis of Souster's way of writing in "Get the Poem Outdoors" and "Flight of the Roller-Coaster" in which language is free to adjust to every nuance of changing events and perceptions. Rhetorical language is the language of "inside" — especially "inside" the formal structures of conventional poetry. "Death on the Construction Site" makes a rhetorically effective statement but it does not create the complex union of subjective response and objective event which Souster achieves elsewhere. Potential subtleties of rhythm, accent and phoneme repetition are eliminated by the force of the rhetorical frame; also eliminated is the accurate perception of subject matter which such complexities of poetic

language require. A rhetorical structure needs only a static response to experience.

Souster also uses clichés to evade a direct reaction to his
subject. These lines occur in his elegy to Karl Polanyi:

> But the things you've done,
> what managed to get written,
> transmitted, spoken here,
> the minds you've helped shape,
> the directions you've charted!
>
> ("At the Polanyi's," *AI* 48–49)

These are from a poem about a jazz musician:

> So I say to you:
> lower your voice,
> sing, croon or whatever
> to me, your one true listener,
> your only believer
> in this roomful of infidels,
>
> . . . .
>
> Be satisfied with one
> true understanding soul
>
> ("Bar with Jazz Piano," *CU* [59])

Neither poem goes beyond the level of platitude ("one true
listener," "the directions you've charted") to the actuality of the
poet's experience or his feelings.

Closely related to his weakness for clichés and rhetoric
(which is itself a kind of syntactic cliché) is Souster's tendency
—unmoved by any flight of rhetoric—to fall into stock
responses and conventional insights. Young girls have "the
freshness of petals / newly opened" ("The Girls of the
Morning," *Y* 14); steaming earth viewed from a hospital
window becomes a "sudden holiness" ("The Sign," *CU* [56]); a
military band inspires these lines:

> I remember
> too many faces
> that marched off behind them

> to anonymous death,
> betrayed by the beat and blare
> of these Devil's instruments
> ("The Parade," *TEYS* 58)

At times these simplistic responses become outright sentimentalities. The unemployed man in "A Week before Christmas" is so overcome by the holiday season's commercial imagery that he must drink beer "all the afternoon" to get back "the heart to go on" (*ALP* 37); a passenger aircraft flying overhead becomes "one of Air Canada's old warrior workhorse Viscounts" ("One of Our Aircraft," *CU* 67). In "The Visit," which recounts the numerous times he has bid farewell to his aging parents, Souster completely abandons his objectivity.

> I weep unashamed
> as the thought wells over:
>
> *one day they'll not*
> *be here to say goodbye!*
> (*L&F* 91)

Souster seems to use stock responses, sentimentality, clichés and rhetorical syntax to retreat from certain areas of experience which he would rather not explore fully. Some of these areas involve subjects like sexuality and mortality. Others involve simplistic conceptions which Souster has been reluctant to surrender. These conceptions include the evil of war and big business, the helplessness of the unemployed, the guilt of middleclass North Americans, the pathos of small animals, the superiority of the past to the present. Often Souster's evasive techniques serve to maintain the contrast between nature and death which is the basis of his poetic vision. They do so by avoiding the consideration of moral complexities which might challenge his binary interpretation.

The final lines of Souster's poems often reveal his desire to avoid going beyond his dichotomous vision. Souster normally gives very close attention to his concluding lines; at their best these lines are succinctly phrased and indicate either a sudden synthesizing perception ("The Hunter") or an additional perception that is both surprising and morally appropriate ("The Six Quart Basket," *ALP* 130). More often, however, these lines appear to be forced attempts by Souster to bring the poem to a conclusion. The last line of a Souster poem frequently contains a gratuitous epithet.

> . . . he'll find a little warmth
> left behind by that arch-betrayer
> old sluggard morning sun.
>
> ("This Last Dying Fly," *TEYS* 27)

These epithets are either inflated or rhetorical, as above, or trite, like the ending to a poem about the felling of two poplar trees.

> Two giants of the earth
> have been struck down, leaving us
> so equally diminished.
>
> ("My Two Poplars," *TEYS* 52)

The shift to epithet is often subsumed within a larger shift towards the end of the poem from concrete to abstract language. "Riding Out" presents a moving account of Souster lying in bed listening wistfully to the sound of passing transcontinental trains. But in the summarial attempt of the final lines the particularity of this experience dissolves into abstractions accompanied by clichés.

> Headlights soaking up
> the mystery ahead, my sleepless giant
> thunders on toward dawn or oblivion.
>
> (*TEYS* 84)

Similarly, "Among the Willows" describes how Souster as a young boy watched couples making love in the bushes and later speared their prophylactics with a stick, but the poem concludes with the abstract comment, "we had that fresh innocence once" (*AI* 97). Ironically, the power of this poem resides in the sexual fascination and voyeuristic excitement it conveys; the claim of "innocence" is at best a surprising conclusion. Other striking examples of poems weakened by concluding abstract comment include "The Embarrassment" (*L&F* 102), "Peace Demonstration, 1967" (*Y* 36–37) and "Christmas Time at the Hospital for Incurables" (*Y* 102).

In the last poem the concluding lines take on the quality of an epigram—that is, the quality of a literary phrase that has been written for its own symmetry and grace rather than for its appropriateness to the context. It is one of Souster's many poems about the hypocrisy of Christmas celebrations, and details the setting up of the tree and the "game" of visiting and gift giving. It concludes when the decorations have been dismantled and the tree stands

> naked, shivering again
> in a world of winters.
>
> (*Y* 100)

The epigrammatic ending is a common feature in Souster's poetry. It works fairly well in "The Eye" (*SP* 89), "Boys and Ducks" (*SP* 57) or "The Ugliest Woman" (*SP* 44). Sometimes, however, the epigram becomes primarily abstract and rhetorical, as in "The Sirens," a surprisingly metaphorical poem about the sirens of Odyssean legend, which concludes,

> see those bodies sinuously beckoning,
> insidious by day, tumultuous by night.
>
> (*AI* 62)

On other occasions the ending is repetitious; "Summer Falling" presents a detailed late summer perception of falling rose petals and then concludes,

> summer falling
> petal by petal
> before my eyes.
>
> (*Y* 13)

The difficulty with this sort of ending is that it adds no new perceptions to the poem. It may contain a surprising linguistic element but when this element fails, as it often does, the perception becomes redundant and predictable.

While we can assume from his habits of concluding a poem that Souster is often content with gratuitous and rhetorical statements and with conventional insights (see also "Washroom Attendant," *L&F* 45; "The Monkey," *SFSG* [31]; or "Death Chant for Mr. Johnson's America," *Y* 28–32), it is not always clear what areas of experience he is attempting to evade or exclude. There are, however, two themes that he clearly avoids. The most obvious is the subject of his own private feelings, joys and tragedies. Souster is almost invariably the observer of external phenomena; his experienced emotions are largely reactions to nonpersonal circumstances: to passing drunks, prostitutes, cripples, birds, baseball players, birch leaves. Some of his strongest poems are those in which he momentarily invades this forbidden area of personal experience, as in "The Hunter" ("wonder what fate she has in store for me"). But the invasion is either superficial, or else it is turned aside by sentimentality ("The Visit") or by abstraction ("The Embarrassment").

Normally Souster shows the reader only external scenes such as the excitement of New Year revelries ("Happy New Year," *GTSW* 42) or "the noise of streetcars" ("Sunday Night Walk," *GTSW* 4); in neither of these examples does Souster say much about how he feels about the girl he is holding. In "Kew Beach Revisited" Souster speaks of "my first big love, / kid stuff, but wonderful" (*Y* 124) but gives no hint of this love's intensity or complexity. As he says himself in one poem,

> I have my own times
> and I keep my sorrows
> carefully to myself,
> so with the years
> they've become an even
> more precious treasure
>
> ("Mourning Dove," *Y* 46)

Too often Souster's poems project a dull, conventional consciousness, afraid to sound its own depths and content to shelter behind external circumstances and commonplace sentiments.

> All that's evil
> hunches outside my window,
> all that's foul
> crouches beside my door.
>
> Great beast of the fog,
> for three days and nights
> I've endured the smell of you,
> . . . .
> grow tired of our curses
> our bored, lifeless faces
>
> ("Great Beast of the Fog," *TEYS* 17)

The attribution of "evil" to the fog here is gratuitous and unsubstantiated. Similarly, the attribution of bestiality is both gratuitous and unspecific as an image. The "curses" of the third stanza raise questions about who is cursing and what is being cursed, but the poem offers no clear answers. Obviously, the "bored, lifeless faces," in combination with the vagueness of the earlier lines, reflect a "bored" and "lifeless" poet, but Souster withholds the reasons why he is "bored" and "lifeless" and substitutes instead an imagistically undistinguished example of the pathetic fallacy.

Sexuality is the other theme which Souster cannot deal with successfully. Although his poems contain an undercurrent of concern with sexual behaviour and sexual expression, none of them present women as feeling, experiencing individuals, nor do they refer to the sexual consummation of love in other than indirect and metaphorical terms. This failure in Souster's poetic vision is not mitigated by his frequent expressions of interest in women and sexuality and of empathy with lovers and their experiences. In many of his love poems Souster prefers to contemplate the woman while she is asleep ("Girl

Asleep," *GTSW* 44; "Asleep," *GTSW* 50; "Dreams Were Always Cheap," *GTSW* 53; "I Sit Down to Write," *ALP* 73; "Caterpillar," *ALP* 81), absent ("Brampton Train Crossing," *CU* 123–26), or otherwise unaware that he is thinking of her ("Study: The Bath," *TSP* 82). Souster's typical point of view correspondingly displays little attention to the feelings or concerns of the woman. His love poems usually focus on phenomena external to both parties ("Happy New Year," *GTSW* 42; "Night Watch," *GTSW* 43; "Sunday Night Walk," *GTSW* 4; "Our World in Winter," *L&F* 20) or on the poet's own feelings of loneliness ("Asleep," "Dreams Were Always Cheap"). On occasion the reality of the woman is evaded through rhetoric (" 'All the Thrones of Their Kingdoms,' " *GTSW* 3) or through metaphor:

> And your eyes shone like phosphorus
> And your lips were ruby caves.
>
> ("Meeting," *GTSW* 36)

Souster's poems about sex are equally indirect. In "Homecoming" the poet returns not to a woman but to "joyful bedsprings" (*CT* 100). In "Migration" lovemaking is described in an elaborate metaphor of a

> . . . sweet curse that sweeps the birds
> up from the golden South
> each false springtime of March,
>
> . . . .
>
> in a devil's vortex of winds and piercing snow,
>
> so that the shoreline's littered and the waters ride
> with ten thousand corpses offered
> to the grinning gods
>
> (*AI* 54)

Like all Souster's associations of sexuality with the "inside" forces of death, this metaphor is deliberately ambiguous.

Souster's poems about sexuality stand in direct contrast to his declared preferences for realistic presentation. The metaphor in "Mira Night," for instance, stands in the place of literal detail.

> O I moved
> from the blaze of your lips
> to the stoked furnace
> of your thighs,
> afterwards stayed
> a long time listening
> to the hammers of our hearts
> sounding fainter, fainter.
>
> (*L&F* 37)

Although here the metaphors are conventional, the physical references ("lips," "thighs") are concrete enough to make the overall effect simply mediocre rather than weak. A similar effect is achieved in "Brampton Train Crossing" in a three-cornered struggle among realistic details, clichés and predictable metaphors.

> Next perhaps the slip
> will drop to the floor, your hands pushing down
> the tight-fitting panties—there, you'll stand free
> as God made you, as your mother and father
> conceived you, . . .
> . . . .
> in all your white womanhood, full orchard
> of your body made for a poet's savouring,
> for poems to be plucked from—melons, grapefuits,
> pears, plums, fruits of all seasons,
> sun-warmed, life-renewing. . . .
>
> (*CU* [125])

As the woman sheds her clothes and makes her physicality more visible, this poem conversely rushes to dress both itself and her in the fig leaves of metaphor. In a poem in which realistic detail is totally absent, as in the following reworking of the "any port in a storm" jest, the result can be not only unconvincing but also unintentionally comic and pretentious:

> I have come into my port again,
> Home from weathering the storms,
>
> . . . .
>
> I have slid into anchor noiselessly,
> And now the waters of your body under me
> Lie still and untroubled, knowing peace,
> And the long voyage is over.
>
> ("In Port," *GTSW* 39)

These several areas of static response to experience, whether to women, to self, or to the natural or humanly created worlds, appear closely related to the uniformity of style and poetic structure which persists throughout the thirty years of Souster's work. During these years there is only one significant stylistic change, the change from an overly rhetorical, declarative voice delivered in relatively long verse lines to a predominantly conversational tone, carefully articulated in brief, precise and imagistic lines. Souster achieved this new style in the early 1950s under the influence of William Carlos Williams. He acknowledged the change in "Some After-thoughts on *Contact* Magazine."

> . . . the next year [1952] something led me back to those two issues [*Origin* nos. 1 and 2, lent to him by Dudek at Charlemagne, Quebec, in 1951] and then Louis came to Toronto in May and left me as a gift *The Collected Later Poems of William Carlos Williams*. From that time on my world assumed its present shape.[3]

However, this new "shape" was static, too, and included the same tendency towards preemptive and artificial termination of poems as Souster's original style. Several critics have noticed the recurrent sentimentality and careless diction which this "shape" could allow. In 1965, Hayden Carruth catalogued numerous failed epigrams, gratuitous emotional declarations and semantic contradictions which flaw Souster's poems, particularly in their conclusions.[4] Almost a decade later, Peter Stevens lamented

> the repetitions, the downright obviousness, the platitudes expressed

in attempts at epigram, the sentimentality, the heavy-handed attacks on gentility, pretentiousness, and the posings of people, more often than not stated in a language unenlivened by a spirited rightness or an exact definition by line or an ironic twist.[5]

All of these criticisms were anticipated by Cid Corman in his letters to Souster from 1953 on. In March 1953, reacting to *Shake Hands with the Hangman* (1953), he notes Souster's difficulty in expressing himself personally in his work and his tendency to self-pity and sentimentality.

A good many of these poems were potentially good ones which you muffed through carelessness or a too early fatigue . . . too easy phrases and conclusions. . . .

Of your weakness, your inability to clarify your emotions, what could be more revealing than a poem like THE TASTE OF THE WAR. Under the rhetorical lies the usual residue of self-pity. And the vagueness! Poems like NE PASSEZ PAS are again cheap. Your last line is cheap, I repeat. It has emotional appeal. Sure. But what is it saying? What does it mean? I just don't follow these kinds of poems. THE POET MUST BE ACCURATE. [6]

In 1955 Corman writes to Souster concerning *For What Time Slays.* Referring to the poem "Two Dead Robins," Corman points out Souster's characteristic drift from the particular to the abstract and sentimental.

I like very much the way you use language here modestly and openly; in fact I envy you your ease; but, the ending I don't see! It evaporates! Is it the genuine response to the event of the burial? It seems to me an *evasion* of poetic *responsibility.* I mean that the first seven lines establish a very particular situation and action; the last two lines amend the action in terms of an apologetic and sentimental reflection.[7]

In 1956 Corman receives a copy of *The Selected Poems,* and his general response, especially to Dudek's editing, is positive. His only reservation again centres on the missed opportunities in many of the poems. "Many of the poems, as always, annoy

me, just because they have power even though you don't do jus-
tice by 'em. "[8] In 1958, however, when he receives *Crepe-Hanger's
Carnival,* Corman again accuses Souster of evasion, sentimentality and extended abstract conclusions.

What I find missing or off are always the same things: sufficient pene-
tration and a mastering sense of shape. You tend toward the rather
pat sentimental close and you often draw a poem out longer than is
necessary.[9]

He has a similar reaction in 1962 to *A Local Pride.*

The weaknesses for me are the old ones. These remain jottings largely
rather than poems. Your feeling for language doesn't go quite deep
enough to resist the content, etc.

Here he appends a rather pointed comment about Souster's
task and potential:

I think you have 5 poems in you to write, with time: one about your
relation to Lee [Souster's wife], one about your relation to your
father, one to Toronto, one to your war experience, and one to
poetry. No hierarchy in the order, but they cannot be easily arrived at
and will not be bluffed through to. I think you will need another 10
years. And a lot of painstaking work. But I feel there is a possibility.
And that's already much.[10]

In 1964 *The Colour of the Times* elicited from Corman a more
balanced response than usual, but he nevertheless repeated his
previous criticisms.

The feeling is frankly sentimental, by and large, but anyhow honest.
And I have no question of it. The poems *do* reflect how you feel. That
you do drop into standard phrases, etc., is unfortunate and yet again
is the way you feel about language. The language moves between a
pseudo-tough (old fashioned hip gab) and a pseudo literary. I like you
best when the words fall between these extremes, simple and full of
breath and ridden out. The end of THE MAN WHO FINDS HIS
SON . . . A THIEF is better perceived and more directly put than is
customary. (You tend at times to be satisfied with much less than
your openings suggest.)[11]

In all these comments it is clear that Corman paid insufficient attention to the strengths of Souster's poetry: namely, his dramatic and unembellished presentation of perceptions, the directness and understatement of his language, and his avoidance of the appearance of artifice through minimal form, colloquial language and nondirective diction and syntax.

Not all of Souster's responses to Corman's letters are currently available. Two of the ones that are available, however, are probably representative. The following is Souster's reply to Corman's remarks about *A Dream That Is Dying:*

Your comments . . . hit the nail on the head more than once.

But I think you expect too much from my poetry. Every person should know their own limitations. The sooner they get to know them the happier they'll be. I know what mine are and I don't stray very much outside them. And one of my limitations is precisely that inner vision, that "bed rock" which you urge me to strive for. I think you either have it or you haven't got it: and I don't think I have. And there's no use straining after it, or trying to fake it up by hiding it behind the language etc. I'm afraid the surface of most things is attractive enough to me — let me lead people to them, make them aware of them — and let them take the deeper meaning as it hits them.[12]

The resignation in this reply contrasts greatly with the irreverent ambition of Souster's editorials in *Direction.* Eight years later, in a response to Corman's evaluation of *A Local Pride,* Souster wrote with marginally more courage, although the modesty and self-deprecation which characterize many of Souster's later self-appraisals are still very much evident.

Appreciate it you laying it on the line re LOCAL PRIDE. I would agree with nearly all of it, but whether I can go beyond my present range only time and hard work will tell. Right now I feel in between periods — as if something new has to come out of it. As to whether I can achieve the depth you would like to have, that is debatable. In many ways I'm still a child, naive, almost always trusting my emotions; maybe I just don't want to look too deep. But I don't think I run away or turn my back on too much. This isn't an easy city or an easy time.[13]

After the dissolution of Contact Press in 1966, Souster did

indeed aspire to "go beyond his present range" in a series of attempts at new forms: the novel, long poem, prose poem and series poem. None of these were more successful than the best of his past work, although a cursory examination of many of them, particularly the novels and the long poems, can help clarify both Souster's major writing weaknesses and his own perceptions of his work's deficiencies.

Souster's aspirations as a novelist consumed most of his writing time between the breakup of Contact Press and the pseudonymous publication of the novel *On Target* in 1973. He wrote at least six drafts of this novel about Royal Canadian Air Force Bomber Command operations in World War II, under such titles as "The Last Year of the War," "Another Time, Another Place," "Something of Eagles," "The Searchlights They Are Blinding Me," "A Time and a Place," "In Air Force Blue" and "Tour of Operations." His motivations for this long period of dedication to a single work were complex. Apart from his obvious desire to enlarge his literary range, Souster appears to have been driven by strong feelings about the Second World War and his minor role in it and also by nostalgia for the "outside" world of youth, sexuality and freedom from inhibition which the war unfortunately appears to have signified for him. Souster's own career in the RCAF was anything but glamourous. On enlistment he was restricted to ground duty because of poor eyesight; a month before the end of the war he was transferred to Europe; on V-E Day he arrived at an operational Bomber Command base. In most of the drafts of *On Target* the protagonist (usually named Bill Sutcliffe) fails pilot training but becomes a bombardier; he is posted to Europe late in the war but in time to experience eighteen missions over Germany and various passionate erotic entanglements. The novel can be read as Souster's projection of what the war could have been for him had his own experiences not been so limited. Souster considered this novel, as he wrote to Corman, "something that had to be done, a debt perhaps to the dead."[14] On 19 July 1970, he describes the project as "a minor obsession," on 19 September as "something I had to do and enjoyed doing," on 4 July 1971, as "my Magnificent Obsession": "this last couple of months everything else has been put aside to enable me to complete the typing of the fourth draft of my Magnificent Obsession, that Air Force novel I've been trying to write for what seems years and years now."[15]

Souster's only previous attempt at a novel, *The Winter of Time*, pseudonymously published in 1949, has none of the compulsive nostalgia of *On Target*. It is a brief work (160 pages), set mainly in the present and the recent past, which attempts to deal "realistically" with the love life of a young Canadian airman who arrives in Europe (like Souster) too late to take an active role in the war. As in all of Souster's attempts at the novel, there is no evident differentiation between the perspective of the main character (Harry Byers) and that of the author. Since Byers is an emotionally immature youth whose overly romantic expectations result either in unrealistic exaltation or in extreme letdown and self-pity, the lack of a separate authorial perspective makes it difficult for a reader to trust the perceptions of the book. The most interesting parts of the novel are cameo portraits of Louis Dudek ("Pete Adams") and Irving Layton ("Walter Green") which Souster awkwardly inserts into the final chapters of a meandering plot.

On Target borrows the first of two major love relationships experienced by Harry Byers in *The Winter of Time*. Harry falls in love "at first sight" with a virginal but passionate English girl, a member of the Woman's Army Air Force; they become mutually orgasmic lovers, marry and separate on his transfer back to Canada; she dies in childbirth during his absence. Souster's attempt to affirm sexuality and passion as "outside" forces is a dominant but unconvincing element in the book. In the 1966–67 drafts Souster elaborates this plot with special attention to its romantic qualities. He also introduces detailed descriptions of eighteen missions which the new protagonist flies over Germany taken from the logbooks and memories of an acquaintance (W.E.A. Servage) and from the official records of the RCAF.

The combat descriptions are the strongest part of the book. Here Souster is doing what he does best—articulating a vision of material reality. His language is direct and factual and makes good use of both technical and colloquial terms for aircraft and armaments. Unfortunately, in the structure of the novel these chapters are merely interludes in a plot which consists mainly of the romantic adventures of Bill Sutcliffe. Like Harry Byers, Sutcliffe is a limited, naive and self-pitying person. Because of Souster's failure to establish a separate literary perspective, Sutcliffe's sentimental and essentially selfish expectations of English women become the chief values asserted by the book.

"Prue," I said, but the door closed at the same moment. The light inside went out almost immediately. It was all over.

I walked slowly back to the car. I still couldn't believe it. Tomorrow I'd wake and find it had only been a bad dream. I had lots of bad dreams these days. This was a bad one, all right, but it was still only a dream. Tomorrow I'd phone Prue up at the chemist's shop. She'd answer and before long her laughter would come rippling across the wire. Every time she laughed like that I felt good all over.

Both of Souster's published novels are limited by simplicities of characterization, by failure to develop the authorial point of view and by an unconvincing presentation of the "outside" theme. Souster's prose style, overly explicit and syntactically conventional sentences that are in sharp contrast to the appositional and informal syntax of most of his better poems, is a further limitation.

Perhaps the risks had never been fully explained, but we'd seen enough British and American war movies to know that death was one of the principal ingredients of war in the air. It was only that I'd never seen a war movie where they showed you a close-up of the hero with one side of his face blown off or horribly burned. So I'd been slightly unprepared when it happened right on my own doorstep. Now that it had happened, though, and I'd handled myself not too badly through it, I could almost think about death objectively, unemotionally. The hell you can, a voice said within me, but I shrugged that voice off. The truth was all very clear now.

(*OT* 85)

During the 1960s Souster made a second serious attempt to

break out of his customary style in his long poem "Death Chant for Mr. Johnson's America," which begins

> America
> you seem to be dying
> America
> moving across the forty-ninth parallel each day a stronger
>   more death-laden stench; wafting inshore from off the
>   Great Lakes the same unmistakable stink, so unlike the
>   usual putrefaction of these waters
> America
> the cracks are beginning to show
> America
> I knew you were marching to doom the night. . . .

(*SP* 91)

The poem continues in much the same rhetorical vein. In his introduction to Souster's *Selected Poems,* Michael Macklem recognizes the limitations of the poem but sees them as indications of a possible new avenue of development for Souster.

"Death Chant" is not a successful poem, perhaps not a poem at all. But it does indicate new possibilities.

(*SP* 23)

In actuality, "Death Chant" is stylistically retrogressive in terms of Souster's overall career. Its rhetoric and its openly sociological concern are limitations that also marred most of the poems in his first two books and which he began to transcend under the influence of Williams and Corman in the early 1950s.

More innovative qualities are present in Souster's prose poems, which begin to appear late in the 1960s, and in his series of poems in *Change-up* called "Pictures of a Long-lost World." What may be the earliest of the prose poems, "What Does It All Mean," an elegy to John Sutherland, possesses the worst qualities of both his prose and poetry: an overly explicit style and a pretentious conclusion.

What does it all mean?

Perhaps if I ever see you alive again you may
have the answer.

(*SFSG* 36)

"The Last Batter" (dated July 1968), which concludes *So Far So Good*, has much of the whimsy of Souster's best work such as "Flight of the Roller-Coaster," but the prose form allows such wasteful uses of language that the poem dissolves into extravagant sentimentality.

... we are all alive in this great empty field of weed-high grass, only the iron girders of the gone-forever grandstand pointing up almost despairingly in the afternoon sunshine, no crowd or crowd-roar, only the endless traffic going by. . . .

(*SFSG* 99)

The advantages of the prose poem are that it allows the poet to escape the habits of normal composition — his conventional choices of line breaks, stanza length, poem length — and to concentrate on exact language and rhythm. Its disadvantage is the one Souster succumbs to above: the poet can forget that he is writing poetry and fall into the inexact diction and loose syntax which are characteristic of bad prose. Souster begins to find the advantages of the prose poem by the early 1970s. "The Stacker" is for the most part precise, concrete and free of the predictable structural qualities of a typical Souster poem.

It's his job, then, to lift the dead bodies up so they form a neat pile on the large flat carts made especially for the purpose. He's a large, heavy man, seems to handle the bodies quite easily. As he picks one up he turns the body so that it rests face down on the pile. Sometimes he doesn't get one placed exactly right, the head sticking out several inches beyond the others; and being the perfectionist he is he'll tug or push that particular body to get it back into line — once he even gives a kick when his hands don't seem to be making the right progress. He's a sensitive man, too, even with day after day of this bloody work; and where a neck shows without a head he'll cover it with a piece of burlap standing by for just such a purpose.

(*SP* 127)

Despite its rambling and highly declamatory conclusion, "The Stacker" is a more impressive achievement than most Souster poems of this period. "Back Lane" (*CU* [17]) is another example of the way a prose poem improved Souster's style.

"Pictures from a Long-lost World" is a series of nineteen poems scattered throughout two volumes: *Change-up* and *Extra Innings*. The series is Souster's only venture into a form which allows the poet to link together similar perceptions which may occur weeks, months or years apart. The common quality of the perceptions in Souster's series is the sense of a critical moment which alters the world irrevocably. The best of these poems are detached and austere in style; they resemble snapshots which preserve the images of moments in human history which can never be redeemed. Poems which have this quality include "Adolph Hitler at the Straits of Dover, 1940" (*CU* [107]), "Wrong Turn at Sarajevo" (*CU* [75]) and "1912":

> The young officers of cavalry
> fresh from Sophia sit stiff-backed on horses
>
> . . . .
> Dead comrades lie at their horses' feet.
> They lie singly or piled together.
> If there's time they'll be buried,
> if not buzzards will strip them clean.
>
> In this year of rapid advances
> nothing is certain.
>
> (*CU* [11])

Yet despite Souster's attempt at a new form, his impulse for nostalgia, for lamenting the loss of a once-present moment, is still strong. Nostalgia is a pervasive quality in all of Souster's writing, in new forms or old. His novels enlarge the world of a postadolescent protagonist and of Souster's own immediate postadolescence. His prose poems lament the passing of the world of his youth in events like the death of John Sutherland and the demolition of Toronto's Maple Leaf Stadium. His poetry generally celebrates the lost world of his youth — green, sexually innocent, romantic. Souster represents the ideal of youth through "unchanging" natural images (trees, birds, clouds or squirrels) or else he fabricates a world of youthful excitement through intense expressions of abstract passion.

Souster's poetry changes remarkably little after the early 1960s. Year after year he attempts to repeat his early experiences. His efforts to break out are almost all attempts to lengthen his world. He tries novels, prose poems, long poems, series poems; but he does not attempt to say or see more than he has said or seen before. When experience resists his efforts to cast it into familiar perceptual moulds, his poems become evasive and end suddenly in vague, formulaic, or gratuitous language. In his poems about women and about sexual love for women, he rarely acknowledges their personal reality but insists instead on casting them into predictable moulds.

In recent books like *Change-up* and *Extra Innings* nostalgia has become Souster's operative poetic vision. His desire to re-live the past requires the constant re-creation of language structures which will sustain images of the past. When new content intrudes, it is transformed into familiar content by the use of rhetoric, cliché, epigram, abstraction. Ironically, Souster's dominating desire to preserve the "outside" and unfettered world of his youth has resulted in a pronounced tendency to rely on the stylistic fetters of conventional or "inside" poetry.

CHAPTER EIGHT

Canadian Modernists

I have raged all my life, with Ezra Pound at my back, shouting "Let's get on with it!"... "Ou Sont les Jeunes?"... Major Canadian Poets — Major Forms of Archaism"! But most writers and artists anywhere are not radical modernists, they're at best milk-and-water derivations.

(Dudek, "The Meaning of Modernism," *TC* 94)

The modernist movement in western art and literature began in Europe and Latin America late in the nineteenth century; it came to England and the United States in 1910–11 with the Post-impressionist Exhibition in London and with the early imagist work of Pound, Ford Madox Ford, T.E. Hulme, Hilda Doo-little and William Carlos Williams. It was a massive movement which contained countless groups and subgroups: symbolists, surrealists, fauvists, futurists, dadaists, postimpressionists, imagists, vorticists, aestheticists, primitivists, constructivists and cubists. It included such diverse writers as Baudelaire, Kafka, Manuel Bandeira, Joyce, Yeats, Woolf, Lawrence, Mann, Beckett, Grass and Pirandello. Modernism in Anglo-American literature was already thirty years old when Louis Dudek and Raymond Souster began writing, but only fifteen years old in Canada. Its influence first appeared in Canada in

1925–26 in the work of A.J.M. Smith during his coeditorship with F.R. Scott of the *McGill Fortnightly Review*. Smith's work, and later that of Ralph Gustafson, P.K. Page and Robert Finch, reflected many of the characteristics of early Anglo-American modernism: the rejection of humanism, of democratic taste, of commercialism, of technology, of verbal imprecision and excess, as well as a preference for the traditional over the contemporary, for order over chance process, for abstraction over realism, for literary detachment over advocacy and for irony and symbol over emotional expressionism. Smith's version of modernism dominated Canadian poetry in the early 1940s, partly through the influence of *Preview* magazine (Sutherland's *First Statement* was the first challenge to the dictums of *Preview*). Internationally, however, the early modernist concern with detachment and with creating abstract patterns rather than portraits of the phenomenal universe had been largely discarded (especially by Pound, Williams, Miller and Lawrence) in favour of a neo-Arnoldian view of the writer as a critic of culture and society and as an artist fully engaged in historical time. The original modernist position was still apparent outside Canada in the New Criticism and in the visual arts, particularly in the reductive and antirealistic work of Picasso, Epstein and Wyndham Lewis.

In the 1940s the contradictions within the modernist movement were represented by Dada's rejection of content and social engagement and Pound's vociferous embracing of them, by Williams's attempts to find value in the present and the colloquial and Eliot's attempts to find it in the traditional and the literary, by Proust's and Stevens's attempts to escape time through the transcendent moment and Pound's attempt to redeem it through the accumulations of art and culture. The situation was further complicated by the impact which social realism had on Western art in the 1930s. Because of its humanist emphasis on the portrayal and criticism of social conditions, social realism resembled the "sensitive" romantic aesthetic which the original modernists had opposed. Nevertheless, it seduced many modernists into declarations of social engagement like A.J.M. Smith's comment, "The artist . . . must be concerned with the world situation in which, whether he likes it or not, he finds himself." [1]

Louis Dudek first entered the modernist debates through social realism, as his early poems in the *McGill Daily* and in *East of the City* attest. His editorials in *First Statement* question the "carvings" of Smith and call for a poetry grounded in "the economic life of the people." [2] When he came under the influence of Lionel Trilling at Columbia University, his political inclinations changed from socialist to elitist, but his sense of literature's involvement in the social order was confirmed. Trilling viewed the writer not only as an Arnoldian "critic of culture" but as an inheritor of humanity's spiritual concerns.

No literature has even been so intensely spiritual as ours. I do not venture to call it religious, but certainly it has the special intensity of concern with the spiritual life which Hegel noted when he spoke of the great modern phenomenon of the secularization of spirituality. [3]

At this time Dudek also became associated with Ezra Pound, and so became influenced simultaneously by Pound's polemical engagement in modern culture and by Trilling's insistence, in defiance of the New Criticism, that the polemical content of a literary work was at least as important as its form.

. . . structures of words they [the modernist writers] may indeed have created, but these structures were not pyramids or triumphal arches; they were manifestly contrived not to be static and commemorative but mobile and aggressive, and one does not describe a quinquireme or a howitzer or a tank without estimating how much *damage* it can do. [4]

These influences were crucial in determining the kind of poetry Dudek would eventually write. For example, his adoption of temporal form in *Europe, En México* and *Atlantis* reflects a rejection of the spatial "time-transcending" form of Eliot and Stevens in favour of the "transcendental realism" [5] he had noted in Proust. His adoption of a relaxed "improvised rhythmical speech"[6] line rather than the sculptural "no superfluous word" line of Eliot reflects his acceptance of temporality as a condition of artistic process and his opposition to the concept of art as "a world beyond appearance" and removed "from the agony of the relative,"[7] a concept argued by such modernist theoreticians as Worringer, Hulme and Ortega. His selection of modernist masters pointedly ignores Hulme and the modernist ideas of "pure" poetry removed from "the transience of the organic,"[8] and unexpectedly includes the humanists Sandburg and Lee Masters and their "real concerns":

> But I go back always to the first free moderns
> > Lawrence, Aldington, Eliot (then), Pound (1915)
> > Lee Masters (yes! Sandburg too)
> for the beginning of what we need: straight language
> > and relevance to our real concerns[9]

Throughout his mature work Dudek has espoused an evolved modernism which seeks a transcendental vision expressed in temporal form and idiom and rooted in the here and now. He makes his primary commitment to historical time and cultural realities. His modernism is humanist in its attachment to contemporary life but antihumanist in its belief in transcendent vision as the ultimate artistic goal.

> What we need is a mean between the positions of T.S. Eliot and Ezra Pound; a view of civilization, art, life, that is both transcendental and humanist at the same time; a "religion" which is not traditional, but a valid extension of knowledge; and an art that is not antiquarian, but creative in accord with that compulsion.[10]
> ... you don't see glory or heaven anywhere, you don't see God or transcendence ... but there is something going on, in the actual. ... [11]

Many of Dudek's literary disagreements can be seen as consequences of his adoption of this particular form of modernism. His dismissal of Smith ("A.J.M. Smith, whose central aim is aesthetic purity, writes in a style somewhat stiffened by the consciousness of literary models"[12]) is largely a dismissal of poetry that aims to be an aesthetic artifact or commodity and avoids engagement in historical time. His rejection of the critical theories of Northrop Frye and of the Canadian "mythopoeic" poets who have been linked to Frye is a rejection of the early modernist urge to transcend temporal reality through what Ortega y Gasset termed the dehumanization and abstraction of the work of art. [13]

I cannot accept the visionary view of literature, that something other than this world is revealed, or some meaning other than that we know by the light of sense and reason is suddenly revealed by an extraordinary experience, and that some such special revelation, and not the light of common day, is the truth about life and art. [14]

For Dudek, Frye's conviction that "abstract story-patterns" behind individual works of literature are of more significance than the individual works themselves is a betrayal of the given world of "perceived things."

Whatever meaning life has, we have to create out of the material given us here. [15]

Dudek's place in the modernist tradition is thus much closer to Williams and the Pound of the later *Cantos* than it is to Eliot, the New Critics, or Pound, Hulme, Aldington and Flint in 1911. He shares with the movement generally its mistrust of mass culture and that culture's bovine acceptance of a "consumer" relationship to art.

From eleven every morning the program reads "Concert,"
but it turned out to be Be-Bop
      exclusively and German *Sehnsucht*
of Nelson Eddy vintage.
      "How about Mozart?
       Or The Messiah"
piped an American collegian.
      "Let's relax!"
The intellectual calibre (high on this voyage)
is about that of the *Sat.Eve.Post*

but as for entertainment the same
does for all "cattle" (the trade name for passengers).
   What does the sea care
regarding the noise we make?

            (*E* 29)

He also shares the usual modernist belief that technology has
dehumanized man, blemished his history and despoiled his
environment. Here is Dudek's description of a street in Rome:

I look at a streetful of blue exhaust,
a wet trail on the sidewalk where somebody pissed
     in the early hours,
or a man with a burlap bag,

since cities are all the same with their modern baggage—
vast accumulations of beaten, bedraggled mankind.

Only the Emperor's men are happy, with knives in their backs,
handing out corn to the people.

The modern world is hungry for gladiators, for ravenous beasts
    fierce with frustration like themselves.

The street rocks with *scavamenti* and gas-smells.

            (*A* 37)

However, Dudek does not seek escape from the phenomenal
world. The literal conditions of historical event must be not
only accepted but recognized as the nearest to ideal possibility
that the universe contains.

Think of the idiots who want a "vision,"
     having the sun-blasted world before their eyes.
It has been given!

            (*A* 99)

   ... paradise is here or it is nowhere ...
   In streets of night and morning,
   and men broken by labour,
   and the mountainous loom of daylight
      filling the dark night.

> Here or nowhere,
> among the people empty of light.
>
> > > *(A* 89)

Dudek's materialist convictions require that he come to terms with time and mutability, the very factors which many modernists such as Hulme, Eliot, Proust and Lewis experienced as the most negative elements in human existence. Modernist lamentation of temporal necessity certainly occurs in Dudek's poetry:

> I know that all experience is only a progress
> > > to some further goal
> never fixed, never final, never to be enjoyed,
> moving always toward what we rarely dreamed, and never
> > > > > understood.
> > > > > > *(A* 141)

Yet his work overall implies that time should be faced either with resignation or with joy in the vitality of change which mutability creates.

> the sea moss thrashes in the brine, and sand bubbles
> or glistens with calcareous triumph
> > > (now! now! now!)
> and the men bring sea-shells to their wives,
> and young girls flash their stiff buttocks
> as the sun strikes the winning nipple —
> now! now! say the strings in singing consummation,
> we have touched the life-giving current,
> > > making a relay!
> Take it from us, you swarming futures.
> Sing, as we now sing!
>
> > > *(EM* 49)

Dudek's awareness of time's passage is accompanied, as in much modernist writing, by a marked dislike of chaotic form, whether in society or in art. While not seeking to desert historical time for such neo-Platonic or neo-Gnostic concepts as Hulme's "absolute values" and "abstract forms" or Frye's "abstract story-patterns," Dudek does seek "form," "ritual," or "a sudden compacting / of thought" as redeeming qualities in otherwise random social, cosmic or artistic events.

> Chatter is like churning water,
>   a formless deformation of words.
>
> Real speech, some eloquence,
>   demands an occasion —
> a ritual. . . .
>
> (*A* 7)

Chaos for Dudek is never, as it was for Hulme, regrettable and unredeemable disorder. Rather it contains potential for action and creativity. It allows for surprise and adventure in all things.

> The multiplicity of chaos, our actual lives
> whatever they are, leaves us
> free to take the pieces, in any order, and move
>   with new desires.
>
> (*A* 9)

The "vaginal" jungle forges its primordial forms out of raw fertility permitted by cosmic disorder. The poem too is an order created from disorder.

> the poem a crystal
>   formed in an empty cave of time.
>
> (*A* 7)

> A poem is like a living animal.
> If you look at any poem really close
> you will discover its anatomy.
>
> Under the skin are veins, tendons, nerves
> that move and hold it together.
>
> (*A* 24)

In Dudek's view the poet has a responsibility to realize from the vast possibilities of historical time some shapely form, much as nature herself creates the orders of leaves and tendons from the "chaos of growing." He could not perceive such a realization in the Contact Press book by Richard Clarke; hence he considered the work chaotic—"bits of commonplace fact floating in the void." Nor could he see it in Souster's *New Wave Canada*, and so he termed much of that work "incredibly boring in its sameness," [16] "reams of incoherent drivel." Making art out of chaos requires a conscious deliberateness; the work must be "given direction and held in control"; it must achieve "the right proportion between abstract ideas ... and the concrete presentations of realities." [17]

These are high expectations of the literary artist. Dudek, like Pound, Eliot, Trilling and Ortega, is thoroughly elitist in his concepts of literary value and talent. For Dudek, the principles of democracy and democratic taste are inimical to great art. At best, democracy works to purge art of its most overrefined and mannered forms.

> ... democracy as a mere leveller
> swept away a lot of decadent rubbish,
> but it does not define the good.
>
> (*A* 39)

Democracy's most significant effects are to reduce men "to pleasure-seeking animals" (*LP* 225) and taste to "an hierarchy of shams."

> An hierarchy of shams must arise, if no other hierarchy can exist. Today we have our "top hit song," "top radio comedians," "top columnists and movies"—that is, the "best" by the standard of democratic vote. In a society given over to undiscriminated pleasure (which the money-ethic finds the easiest and simplest merchandise), entertainment becomes a field for "popular artists" whose superiority is measured by the "box-office."
>
> (*LP* 227)

Democratization corrupts nonpopular literature as well by preventing "discrimination" and obscuring "the excellent things" with overpraised "rotten work." When interviewed in

1975 by Michael Darling, Dudek spoke at length about this phenomenon and repeated some of his earlier criticisms of Richard Clarke and the poets of *New Wave Canada*.

LD: ... our modernism, our realism, has descended into a kind of slovenliness, and shapelessness, and self-indulgence that is most unfortunate. And this stuff has been subsidized to such an extent that there's too much of it. ... there's a need for discrimination in all this new activity. ... I would like to see critics in action who would pick out the excellent things and the individuals who would eventually go on. ...

But when you see rotten work touted up and overpraised and promoted everywhere, that isn't good for literature, it doesn't make for a great epoch.

MD: You're an elitist, then?

LD: Oh, I damn well am an elitist! You know, there is a very, very cruel fact about this game — that in literature you either have it or you don't have it. ... [18]

Such opinions had little appeal for Raymond Souster either in the early years when Dudek was urging a special Pound issue of *Contact* or in the last years of Contact Press when Souster was supporting Clarke and the *New Wave Canada* poets. Souster's only direct connection to the modernist movement was through imagism and William Carlos Williams; he had little sympathy for its restrained and austere language which he termed "Ezra Pound cold," or for its suspicion of mass culture. While he instinctively shared Dudek's distaste for "commodity" art, his faith in the future rested on the exemplary force of ordinary man, everyday experiences and colloquial language, rather than on the didactic force of a noncommunal elite. His letters reveal that he did not enjoy reading Pound, Joyce, Eliot or Proust; he admired but could not fully understand Charles Olson and Paul Blackburn; he was most comfortable with the work of Williams, Kenneth Patchen and Cid Corman.

Moreover, Souster's intuitive aesthetic was romantic realism, the antithesis of modernism. Romantic realism is the aesthetic which Ortega attributed to "man in general," the common person with whom Souster throughout his work declares sympathy.

> What is it the majority of people call aesthetic pleasure? . . . The answer is easy. A man likes a play when he has become interested in the human destinies presented to him, when the love and hatred, the joys and sorrows of the personages so moves his heart that he participates in it all as though it were happening in real life. [19]

His poems seldom aspire to the transcending stillness of "pure poetry" or to the intellectual didacticism of Pound or Dudek; what they demand of the reader is an active, empathetic response that does not respond to poetry as art but enters into its very composition as "a fiction of human realities." [20] This is as true of the early poems about wartime death ("Postscript," *WWAY* [24]) and love ("Ersatz," *WWAY* [25]) as it is of his later poems about adult experiences, such as "The Embarrassment" (*L&F* 102) or "To My Cat, Minou, Murdered by a Neighbour":

> . . . it was about here
> you must have yawned
> (warm fur of your body
> curled tight in my right arm)
> and I yawned back at once in agreement,
>
> and lowering you to the floor
> walked across and turned off the TV set
> after which we both moved through the house
> to the back door. . . .
>
> (*CU* [49])

Souster's two novels are based entirely on the aesthetics of empathy. Most of the effect of the writing is directed towards making the reader accept and share either the terrors of aerial warfare or the banal attitudes and trivial sexual entanglements of the young male protagonists.

She had an unusually slender waist for such well-proportioned thighs and buttocks, and my hand wouldn't begin to reach around one of her breasts. I was primed like a bull by now and made the most of it with her caressing fingers and earthy whispers in my ear. Once locked in I fought the good fight to burst finally to freedom in one straining, glorious upheaval. . . .

(*OT* 145–46)

The didactic elements in Souster are invariably implicit rather than explicit and are connected to passages of social realism — basically factual portrayals of people or events "enhanced" by the intensification of particular details. These include his portraits of beggars, cripples, prostitutes and the working poor.

> In winter
> You curse the cold, huddled in your coat from the wind,
> You fry in summer like an egg hopping on a griddle,
> And always the whining voice, the nervous-flinging arms,
> The red face, the shifting eyes watching, waiting
> Under the grimy cap. . . .
>
> ("Downtown Corner News-stand," *TSP* 71)

The technical elements of the poem — alliteration, simile, syntactic repetition — are employed to intensify the emotional elements in the presentation and to evoke compassion for the human reality it contains. The aesthetic reality of the poem is underplayed; the figure portrayed is intended to have a greater impact on the reader than the portrait itself.

Souster seldom makes any fine distinction between realism and imagism. For the Imagist movement, the image was a means of arresting phenomenal process, of transcending the contingencies of historical time. "An 'Image,'" Pound wrote, "is that which presents an intellectual and emotional complex in an instant of time. . . . It is the presentation of such a 'complex' instantaneously which gives that sense of sudden liberation; that sense of freedom from time and space limits. . . . "[21] Except for a few instances such as "The Six Quart Basket" and "Study: The Bath," imagism has been for Souster mostly a technique for reducing wordiness and sentimentality, for increasing concreteness and precision of language and for minimizing his own interventions into the text.

> After the fire in the tenement
> Besides the four well-stuffed closets of garbage,
> The six-dozen wine bottles,
> Eighteen gas-cookers, seven woodburning stoves,
>
> Three charred bodies found in a room,
> Which made it a little embarrassing
> Because not even the landlady
> Could remember their names.
>
> ("The Fire in the Tenement," *TSP* 124)

In technique, aesthetic and sensibility, Souster is a romantic realist who employs many of the teachings of modernism to avoid didacticism and excess and to involve the reader in the interrelating and interpreting of a poem's elements. Emotional detachment becomes a technique for allowing the reader to experience emotions freely in response to immediate perceptions. Direct language often becomes the language of particular social types such as the "common man," the prostitute or the amateur baseball player. The poetry also implies the superiority of their social perspectives.

Many of Souster's attitudes and feelings are, however, congruent with those of Dudek and similar to those found throughout modernist writing. As we have seen, Souster is extremely suspicious of commercialism. But the testimony of poems such as "The Launching" (*ALP* 124), "The Pen and Ink Clerks" (*CU* 69) and "Office Death" (*CU* [109–110]) suggests that he does not see the evils of commercialism as Dudek does, as by-products of democracy, but rather as consequences of the common person's oppression by an oligarchy of bankers, businessmen and politicians. Souster's view, as chapter 6 proposes, is Marxist rather than modernist.

Souster also shares the modernist's fear of time and process. He dislikes the changes which technology and urbanization are effecting on the Canadian landscape, and in his work he hearkens back to an earlier era in Toronto ("The Last

Batter," *SP* 112–14; "Shoe Store," *SP* 106–7; "Armadale Avenue
Revisited," *SP* 80–81), to an earlier era in Ontario ("On the
Rouge," *SP* 83) or to his own childhood ("Dominoes," *CU* [38]).
Because of this nostalgia, he writes poems about youthful
romances and wartime adventures thirty years after the fact;
many of these poems seem like attempts to roll back time for his
own satisfaction in the way that his series, "Pictures from a
Long-lost World," attempts to turn the clock back for Western
culture. One of the most curious of Souster's time-resisting
poems is "Lagoons: Hanlan's Point." At its most obvious level,
it is a realistic evocation of childhood experience.

> Mornings
> Before the sun's liquid
> Spilled gradually, flooding
> The island's cool cellar,
> There was the boat
> And the still lagoons,
> With the sound of my oars
> The only intrusion

It is also a clear affirmation of the value of primeval nature
undisturbed by urbanization.

> The only intrusion
> Over cries of birds
> In the nearby shallows
> Or the loud thrashing
> Of the startled crane
> Rushing the air.

But the imagery which Souster employs to intensify this voyage
of "a small boy / ... Moving in wonder / Through the
antechambers / Of a waking world" suggests more profound
meanings. The imagery is openly sexual; it describes a voyage
through layers of consciousness as well as a journey through
layers of memory and history.

> ... in one strange
> Dark, tree-hung entrance,

> I followed the sound
> Of my heart all the way
> To its reed-blocked ending

At this level the poem communicates rejections of mortality and sexuality as well as a rejection of time: "Before the sun's liquid / Spilled gradually, flooding / The island's cool cellar." The sheltering lagoon is here a maternal constant "probed" by the masculine sun and from which a mortal boy must grow. The lagoon itself remains "below" the surface of time; those who drop out of time can pleasantly return to it. The echoes in this area of the poem are both romantic — compare Scott's "The Piper of Arll" and Roberts's "The Gravedigger" — and modernist — Smith's "The Mermaid" or P.K. Page's "Boy with a Sea Dream."

> When the sun came
> To probe the depths
> Through a shaft of branches,
> I saw the skeletons
> Of brown ships rotting
> Far below in their burial ground,
> And wondered what strange fish
> With what stranger colours
> Swam through these places
> Under the water. . . .
>
> (*TSP* 51)

Similar maternal overtones are attached to most of the "outside" images in Souster's work: nature, love, childhood, friendly buildings. These act as refuges for him from the "inside" forces of time, business, urbanization, commercialism, politics, sexuality and mortality. Given these maternal overtones, it is perhaps not surprising that sexuality appears in Souster's poems — as it also does in Eliot's *Waste Land* — as a disruptive "inside" force associated more with guns and prostitution than with love. Souster indeed has a modernist antipathy towards disorder, and this antipathy is directed towards many of the bêtes noires of modernism: the city, capitalism, philistinism, war, sexuality, technology and time. But Souster's positive values are not at all modernist. Rather than Pound's,

Eliot's and Dudek's yearnings for the traditional, the well-crafted and the civilized, or Dada's and Lawrence's yearnings for the primitive and the passionate, Souster expresses a somewhat vague, sentimental, subjective wish for a pastoral and communal world of protected squirrels, groundhogs and starlings, of contented children, happy lovers and unspoiled landscapes. It is this pastoral impulse which is most characteristic of Souster and which distinguishes him most clearly from his contemporaries.

Souster's peculiar combination of pastoralism and romantic realism and Dudek's insistence on the "functionality" and cultural responsibility of poetry were unanticipated in Canadian modernism. Their effect was not to reshape the modernist movement in Canada completely but to expand and update it, making it possible for the first time for sharply contrasting varieties of modernism to coexist and thrive. In the early stages of Dudek's and Souster's careers, the most influential Canadian poets were either formalists — Smith, Finch, Le Pan, Page, Gustafson, Reaney, Pratt — or social realists with some formalist sympathies — Scott, Birney and Livesay. The predominant aesthetic assumptions were either the neo-Platonic theories of Worringer and Hulme *circa* 1908-15 or Stalinist theory of the 1930s. In their various editorial ventures, Dudek and Souster encouraged varieties of neo-Platonic modernism, most notably Page, Phyllis Webb, Leonard Cohen, Eli Mandel, Margaret Atwood and D.G. Jones; they encouraged social realists such as F.R. Scott and Milton Acorn; at the same time they insisted that Canadian writing reconnect itself to the mainline of Anglo-American modernism — Pound, Williams, Blackburn, Olson, Corman — that had evolved from the neo-Platonism of the 1908-15 period. In their poetry they established the credibility of colloquial speech as an alternative to the languages of fin de siècle romanticism and impersonal modernism.

To a degree, Louis Dudek and Raymond Souster undoubtedly influenced contemporary trends in Canadian literature. Through Contact Press they introduced Canadian writers who for the most part (a notable exception is Margaret

Atwood) were realistic in presentation, colloquial in idiom and "engaged" in tone; many of these writers—Nowlan, Acorn, Purdy, Newlove, Bowering, MacEwen—have had widely ranging careers after Contact Press published their work. The popularity of Souster's poetry, anthologized in nearly every school text of modern Canadian writing and published in numerous "selected" editions, has also influenced the modern Canadian sense of what a poem can be—colloquial, realistic, imagistic and minimal in either subject or form. Dudek, seldom anthologized, has not reached or sought a wide audience. His work in the long, temporally structured and reflective poem—in its time unique in Canadian poetry—has, however, had a variety of conscious or unconscious successors: Glassco's *Montreal*, Lee's *Civil Elegies*, Bowering's *Sitting in Mexico* and *Rocky Mountain Foot*, Marlatt's *Steveston*, Newlove's "The Pride," Purdy's *In Search of Owen Roblin* and *On the Bearpaw Sea*. Whatever the exact extent of their influence, Dudek and Souster together helped enlarge, enrich and modernize Canadian literary perspectives.

Notes

Chapter One

1. Audrey Sutherland in an interview with Robert Campbell. Quoted in Robert Campbell, "A Study of the History and Development of Raymond Souster's 'Direction,' 'Contact' and 'Combustion'" (Master's thesis, University of New Brunswick, 1969), p. 20.

2. Souster's father had worked in junior positions at the Standard Bank of Canada and the Canadian Bank of Commerce, from which he retired in 1959. Souster accepted employment as a teller at the Imperial Bank of Canada; at the time of writing he is a custodian of securities at the head office of the Canadian Imperial Bank of Commerce.

3. Souster had hoped for a flight crew posting but failed the physical examination, largely because of poor eyesight.

4. While at this agency, Dudek started an in-house little magazine with the French-Canadian novelist Yves Theriault as coeditor. Dudek recalls, "He and I shared an office in The Canadian Advertising Agency (Sun Life Building) as copywriters. He was writing stories, I was writing poetry, so we started a little agency 'house organ' as they used to call it, but really just a literary outlet for ourselves. No copies of this exist as far as I know, unless Theriault has one" (letter to Frank Davey, 24 October 1974).

5. 1, no. 16: 2-3.

6. 2, no. 8: 17-20. Reprinted in Dudek and Michael Gnarowski, eds., *The Making of Modern Poetry in Canada* (Toronto: Ryerson Press, 1967), pp. 104-6; and in Dudek, *Selected Essays and Criticism* (Ottawa: Tecumseh Press, 1978), pp. 1-3.

7. Quoted by William Goldberg in "The Beginning," a letter in *Direction* 1 (December 1943): 1.

8. Ibid.

9. "Why a New Magazine," *First Statement* 1, no. 2: 1. Reprinted in Sutherland, *Essays, Controversies and Poems*, ed. Miriam Waddington (Toronto: McClelland & Stewart, 1972), p. 21.

10. Sutherland, "Notes on a National Literature," *First Statement* 1, no. 4. Reprinted in *Essays, Controversies and Poems*, pp. 21-22.

11. Work by Layton first appeared in *First Statement* in vol. 1, no. 9 (December 1942), Dudek in vol. 1, no. 10 (January 1943) and Souster in vol. 1, no. 11 (January 1943). During this period, possibly because of Layton and Dudek, Sutherland's aims changed from representing "the various types of writing in Canada" (1, no. 4) to the attacking of "colonialism" and cosmopolitanism (2, no. 4; 3, no. 6), and ultimately to the championing of a "Canadian point of view" and "colloquial language" which characterized his introduction to *Other Canadians* (Montreal: First Statement Press, 1947). Dudek theorizes that Sutherland's literary conservatism in the 1950s was a reversion to the eclecticism of the early issues of *First Statement* (*The Golden Dog* 4 (November 1974): 1-3).

12. "A Retrospect," *The Literary Essays of Ezra Pound* (London: Faber & Faber, 1954), p. 12.

13. T.E. Hulme, "Humanism and the Religious Attitude," *Speculations* (New York, 1924), p. 53.

14. "A Rejected Preface to *New Provinces*, 1936," *Canadian Literature* 24 (Spring 1965): 8. Reprinted in A.J.M. Smith, *Towards a View of Canadian Letters* (Vancouver: University of British Columbia Press, 1973), p. 172.

15. Hulme, "Humanism and the Religious Attitude," p. 53.

16. Sutherland, "Toward a Canadian Realism," *First Statement* 2, no. 5. Reprinted in *Essays, Controversies and Poems*, p. 35.

17. Sutherland, Introduction to *Other Canadians* (Montreal: First Statement Press, 1947). Reprinted in Dudek and Gnarowski, eds., *The Making of Modern Poetry in Canada*, p. 59; and in Sutherland, *Essays, Controversies and Poems*, p. 55.

18. "Introduction to *Other Canadians*," *Essays, Controversies and Poems*, p. 52.

19. Interview with John Nause and J. Michael H. Heenan, *Tamarack Review* 69 (Summer 1976): 31.

20. Sutherland gave up his undergraduate studies at McGill to found *First Statement* and subsequently made it, First Statement Press, and *First Statement*'s successor, *Northern Review*, his life's work. Despite suffering from tuberculosis, he supported his family and his publishing through a long series of part-time jobs.

21. Goldberg, "The Beginning."

22. See William Goldberg, "Open Letter from the Editor to His Reader," *Direction* 7: 1, and the advertisement for "The Poems of Raymond Souster," *Direction* 7: 2 — a book to be published "early in 1946" by "The Cyclic Press."

23. Interview with Frank Davey, Montreal, 15 July 1974.

24. The only known surviving copy of *New Poems* is in the private collection of Professor Michael Gnarowski of Carleton University. Two other chapbooks are announced on the last page of *New Poems*: "The Girl in the Iron Lung" and "The Diary of a Young Man," both by Souster. These were apparently never published.

25. Interview, 15 July 1974.

26. See *D/k*, Dudek's collection of his letters from Ezra Pound, with annotations summarizing the content of his replies (Montreal: DC Books, 1975).

27. Dudek describes this project in *D/k*: "After the conversation with Rudd Fleming in Washington I had started a poetry newsletter to be circulated among a dozen or so poets. Each fellow added his own work and criticism to the file and mailed the folio to the next man on the list. Among the dozen or so participants were William Carlos Williams, Ezra Pound, Rudd Fleming, Paul Blackburn, Raymond Souster. It came to an end when Blackburn's cat mistook the heap of papers for a litter and 'passed judgment' on our labours."

28. Letter from Souster to Dudek, 19 November 1950; in Dudek's private possession.

29. "Some Afterthoughts on *Contact* Magazine," in Michael Gnarowski, ed., *Contact* 1952–54: *Notes on the History and Background of the Periodical and an Index* (Montreal: Delta Canada, 1966), p. 1.

30. Letter to Dudek, 19 November 1950; ms. in Dudek's private possession.

31. Letter to Dudek, 23 June 1951; ms. in Dudek's private possession.

32. Letter to Souster, 17 July 1951; ms. in the collection of Lakehead University Library.

33. Letter to Souster, 11 December 1951; ms. in the collection of Lakehead University Library.

34. This list of participants is taken from Dudek's personal archives. Souster had failed in an attempt at a similar project in the spring of 1951, probably due to his limited number of acquaintances among Canadian writers. See his letter to Dudek, 23 June 1951.

35. Letter to Dudek, 6 October 1951; ms. in Dudek's private possession.

36. Letters to Souster, 11 October 1951 and 26 November 1951; mss. in collection of Lakehead University Library.

37. Letter to Souster, 16 January 1952; ms. in collection of Lakehead University Library.

38. Letter to Souster, 3 February 1952; ms. in collection of Lakehead University Library.

39. Letter to Souster, 7 June 1951; ms. in collection of Lakehead University Library.

40. Letter to Dudek, 23 June 1951; ms. in Dudek's private possession.

41. p. 19. Reprinted in Dudek and Gnarowski, eds., *The Making of Modern Poetry in Canada*, p. 60.

42. "Academic Literature," *First Statement* 2, no. 8. Reprinted in *Selected Essays and Criticism*, p. 3.

43. Letter from Corman to Souster, 3 March 1952; ms. in collection of Lakehead University Library.

44. Letter from Corman to Souster, 12 March 1952; ms. in collection of Lakehead University Library.

45. Letter from Corman to Souster, 15 February 1952; ms. in collection of Lakehead University Library.

46. Letter to Souster, 10 March 1952; ms. in collection of Lakehead University Library.

47. Letter to Souster, 6 May 1952; ms. in collection of Lakehead University Library.

48. Letters from Corman to Souster, 11 August 1952 and 18 September 1952. Dudek discusses the proposal in a letter to Souster dated 9 September 1952. Mss. of all letters in collection of Lakehead University Library.

49. *"Origin* Returns," *Delta* 15: 4.

50. Letter to Souster, 11 November 1952; ms. in collection of Lakehead University Library.

51. Ms. in collection of Lakehead University Library.

52. "The Making of *CIV / n*," in Michael Gnarowski, *Index to CIV / n* (privately published, n.d.), p. 3.

53. *D / k*, p. 103.

54. Letter from Souster to Dudek, undated (circa July 1953); ms. in Dudek's private possession.

55. Mss. in collection of Concordia University Library.

56. Ms. in collection of Lakehead University Library.

57. Letter to Layton, 17 February 1952. Ms. in collection of Concordia University Library.

58. Ms. in collection of Lakehead University Library.

59. Interview with Frank Davey, 26 October 1974.

60. Letter to Souster, 3 February 1952; ms. in collection of Lakehead University Library.

61. Ms. in collection of Concordia University Library.

62. Letter to Souster, 22 March 1952; ms. in collection of Lakehead University Library.

63. Letter to Souster, 2 April 1952; ms. in collection of Lakehead University Library.

64. Letter to Souster, 18 March 1952; ms. in collection of Lakehead University Library.

65. (Toronto: Ryerson Press and Contact Press, 1960), p. 139.

66. A copy of this mimeographed pamphlet is in the Contact Press Collection of the Thomas Fisher Rare Book Library, University of Toronto.

67. Letter to Souster, 18 May 1955; ms. in collection of Lakehead University Library.

68. Letter to Souster, 9 February 1958; ms. in Contact Press Collection, Thomas Fisher Library.

69. Letter from Dudek to Souster, 16 April 1952; ms. in collection of Lakehead University Library.

70. Letter from Dudek to Miller, 29 September 1961; ms. in Contact Press Collection, Thomas Fisher Library.

71. Letter from Miller to Dudek, 5 February 1962; ms. in Contact Press Collection, Thomas Fisher Library.

72. Letter from Dudek to Miller, 8 February 1962; ms. in Contact Press Collection, Thomas Fisher Library.

73. Contact Press Collection, Thomas Fisher Library.

74. Letter from Dudek to Miller, 11 November 1961; ms. in Contact Press Collection, Thomas Fisher Library.

75. Letter to Dudek, 21 March 1963; ms. in Contact Press Collection, Thomas Fisher Library.

76. Letter from Dudek to Miller, 11 June 1962; ms. in Contact Press Collection, Thomas Fisher Library.

77. Letter from Dudek to Miller, 30 September 1964; ms. in Contact Press Collection, Thomas Fisher Library.

78. Letter from Souster to Dudek, 4 October 1964; ms. in Contact Press Collection, Thomas Fisher Library.

79. Since 1956 Dudek had also been editing and personally funding the McGill Poetry Series, a series of poetry chapbooks by McGill

students. He had begun this series because Leonard Cohen wished immediate publication of his first book, *Let Us Compare Mythologies*. Because of editorial conflicts, all that Contact Press could offer Cohen was inclusion in Souster's *Poets 56* anthology.

80. Letter from Dudek to Souster, 15 October 1964; ms. in Contact Press Collection, Thomas Fisher Library.

81. *The First Person in Literature* (Toronto: CBC Publications, 1967), p. 66.

82. Letter from Dudek to Miller, 13 January 1965; ms. in Contact Press Collection, Thomas Fisher Library.

83. Letter from Dudek to Souster and Miller, 30 March 1965; ms. in Contact Press Collection, Thomas Fisher Library.

84. Letter from Souster to Dudek, 3 April 1965; ms. in Contact Press Collection, Thomas Fisher Library.

85. Letter from Miller to Souster and Dudek, 15 September 1966; ms. in Contact Press Collection, Thomas Fisher Library.

86. Letter from Dudek to Souster, 25 September 1966; ms. in Contact Press Collection, Thomas Fisher Library.

87. Ms. in Contact Press Collection, Thomas Fisher Library.

88. Letter from Dudek to Souster, 5 November 1966; ms. in Contact Press Collection, Thomas Fisher Library.

89. Letter to Souster, 6 January 1957; ms. in collection of Lakehead University Library.

90. Letter to Souster, 25 October 1960; ms. in collection of Lakehead University Library.

91. Letter from Dudek to Souster, 26 July 1957; ms. in collection of Lakehead University Library.

92. Letter from Dudek to Souster, 22 August 1958; ms. in collection of Lakehead University Library.

93. *Delta* 24: 24.

94. Letter from Souster to Corman, 24 December 1965; ms. in collection of the Humanities Research Center, University of Texas at Austin.

95. "Get the Poem Outdoors," *So Far So Good* (Ottawa: Oberon Press, 1969), p. [66].

96. *Delta* 15: 4.

97. Letter to Souster, 11 August 1957; ms. in collection of Lakehead University Library.

98. Letter to Peter Miller, 11 June 1962; ms. in Contact Press Collection, Thomas Fisher Library.

99. Ms. in collection of Concordia University Library.

100. Mss. in collection of Lakehead University Library.

101. Letter from Souster to Corman, 31 January 1971; ms. in collection of the Humanities Research Center, University of Texas at Austin.

102. Ms. in collection of Lakehead University Library.

103. Souster, in interview with Robert Campbell. Quoted in Campbell, "A Study of the History and Development of Raymond Souster's 'Direction,' 'Contact' and 'Combustion,'" p. 126.

104. In his letter of 6 October 1951, announcing to Dudek the founding of *Contact*, Souster declares, "MAKE IT NEW is our unofficial slogan." Dudek replies on 11 October, "You astound me with the 'unofficial slogan.' For some time I've been talking... about sometime starting a mag with the NAME: MAKE IT NEW. You took the words out of my mouth. Why not? It would be better than CONTACT. At [*sic*] would also be a name on a new principle; a blasted Verb in it; a whole policy.
    AS THE SUN MAKES IT NEW
    DAY BY DAY MAKE IT NEW
    YET AGAIN MAKE IT NEW.
... Goddam it, it's really what Canada needs." Ms. of Souster letter is in Dudek's private possession; ms. of Dudek's in the collection of Lakehead University Library.

Chapter Two

1. Letter to Souster, 11 October 1951; ms. in the collection of Lakehead University Library.

2. 11 December 1951; ms. in collection of Lakehead University Library.

3. "The Little Mag," in John Glassco, ed., *English Poetry in Quebec* (Montreal: McGill University Press, 1965), p. 60.

4. Letter to Souster, 18 March 1952; ms. in collection of Lakehead University Library.

5. "Academic Literature," *First Statement* 2, no. 8 (1944): 17-20. Reprinted in *Selected Essays and Criticism* (Ottawa: Tecumseh Press, 1978), pp. 1-3.

6. "The Psychology of Literature," paper delivered to the CCTE convention, Saskatoon, August 1974. Reprinted in *Selected Essays and Criticism*, p. 369.

7. "The Little Mag," in Glassco, ed., *English Poetry in Quebec*, p. 60.

8. *Cerberus* (Toronto: Contact Press, 1952), p. 13. Reprinted in *Selected Essays and Criticism*, pp. 27-28.

9. "Ou sont les jeunes?" *Contact* 1, no. 1 (January 1952). Reprinted in *Selected Essays and Criticism*, p. 25.

10. "Censorship and Ideology," *Afterimage* 5 (Spring 1974): 23.

11. "The Sculpture of Poetry," *Canadian Literature* 30 (Autumn 1966): 27.

12. Ibid., p. 30.

Chapter Three

1. "Poet as Philosopher," *Canadian Literature* 53 (Summer 1972): 23.

2. "The Sculpture of Poetry," *Canadian Literature* 30 (Autumn 1966): 32.

Chapter Four

1. *Tamarack Review* 69 (Summer 1976): 13.

2. "The Transition in Canadian Poetry," *Culture* 20 (September 1959): 288-89. Reprinted in Dudek, *Selected Essays and Criticism* (Ottawa: Tecumseh Press, 1978), pp. 128-29.

3. "The Transition in Canadian Poetry," *Selected Essays and Criticism*, p. 126.

4. "The Significance of Lampman," *Culture* 28 (March 1957): 278. Reprinted in *Selected Essays and Criticism*, p. 66.

5. "The Transition in Canadian Poetry," *Selected Essays and Criticism*, p. 129.

6. "The Significance of Lampman," *Selected Essays and Criticism*, p. 66.

7. Ibid.

8. Ibid., p. 67.

9. Ibid., p. 75.

10. "The Transition in Canadian Poetry," *Selected Essays and Criticism*, p. 131.

11. "E.J. Pratt: Poet of the Machine Age," *Tamarack Review* 6 (Winter 1958): 79. Reprinted in *Selected Essays and Criticism*, pp. 120–21.

12. "Literature in English," in J.M.S. Careless and R. Craig Brown, eds., *The Canadians, 1867–1967* (Toronto: Macmillan, 1967), p. 651. Reprinted in *Selected Essays and Criticism*, p. 232.

13. "The Transition in Canadian Poetry," *Selected Essays and Criticism*, pp. 131–32.

14. Ibid., p. 133.

15. Ibid., p. 126.

16. "Art, Entertainment and Religion," *Queen's Quarterly* 70, no. 3 (Autumn 1963): 426–27.

17. "Patterns of Recent Canadian Poetry," *Culture* 19 (December 1958): 411. Reprinted in *Selected Essays and Criticism*, p. 106.

18. "Patterns of Recent Canadian Poetry," *Selected Essays and Criticism*, p. 102.

19. "Literature in English," *Selected Essays and Criticism*, p. 233.

20. "Patterns of Recent Canadian Poetry," *Selected Essays and Criticism*, pp. 96–97.

21. Ibid., p. 98.

22. "Literature in English," *Selected Essays and Criticism*, p. 232.

23. Ibid.

24. "The Psychology of Literature," paper delivered to the CCTE convention, Saskatoon, August 1974. Included in *Selected Essays and Criticism*, pp. 373–74.

25. Ibid., p. 377.

26. Interview with John Nause and J. Michael H. Heenan, *Tamarack Review* 69 (Summer 1976): 33.

27. "Trouncing the Younger Poets," *Canadian Literature* 34 (Autumn 1967): 84.

28. *Tamarack Review* 69 (Summer 1976): 11-12.

29. Interview with Nause and Heenan, p. 32.

30. "The Psychology of Literature," *Selected Essays and Criticism*, p. 372.

31. "Art, Entertainment, and Religion," pp. 428-29.

32. Ibid., p. 423.

33. Charles Olson, "Projective Verse," *Human Universe* (New York: Grove Press, 1967), p. 52.

34. *Selected Essays and Criticism*, p. 101.

35. "The Psychology of Literature," *Selected Essays and Criticism*, p. 369.

36. *Delta* 22 (October 1963): 25.

37. 6 August 1966, p. 24.

38. 8 April 1967, p. 28.

39. P. 428.

40. "The Transition in Canadian Poetry," *Selected Essays and Criticism*, p. 134.

41. "Patterns of Recent Canadian Poetry," *Selected Essays and Criticism*, pp. 101-2.

42. Ibid., p. 106.

43. Letter to Souster, 5 November 1966; ms. in Contact Press Collection, Thomas Fisher Library.

44. Letter to Souster, 25 September 1966; ms. in Contact Press Collection, Thomas Fisher Library.

45. "Trouncing the Younger Poets," p. 83.

46. "Lunchtime Reflections on Frank Davey's Defence of the Black

Mountain Fort," *Tamarack Review* 36 (Summer 1965): 63. Reprinted in *Selected Essays and Criticism*, p. 212.

47. *Books in Canada*, October 1978, p. 37.

48. "Wonder Merchants: Modernist Poetry in Vancouver during the 1960s," *Godawful Streets of Man, Open Letter* 3, no. 6 (Winter 1976–77): 191.

49. *Canadian Literature* 22 (Autumn 1964): 39. Reprinted in *Selected Essays and Criticism*, pp. 197–98.

50. Interview with Nause and Heenan, p. 33.

51. Ibid., pp. 32–33.

52. Interview with Michael Darling, *Essays on Canadian Writing* 3 (Fall 1975): 12.

53. Interview with Nause and Heenan, p. 39.

54. Ibid.

Chapter Five

1. Letter to Corman, 24 December 1965; ms. in collection of the Humanities Research Center, University of Texas at Austin.

2. Preface to *New Wave Canada* (Toronto: Contact Press, 1966).

3. Letter to Earle Birney, 15 October 1951; ms. in the Earle Birney papers, Thomas Fisher Rare Book Library, University of Toronto.

Chapter Six

1. Robert Fulford, "On Raymond Souster: A Good Toronto Poet Toronto Never Discovered," *Maclean's* 77, no. 8 (18 April 1964). Reprinted in Dudek and Gnarowski, eds., *The Making of Modern Poetry in Canada* (Toronto: Ryerson Press, 1967), p. 245.

2. Peter Stevens, "Souster's Vision of Life So Consistent," *Globe and Mail*, 6 December 1975.

3. "Souster, Rooted and Faithful, in His Sufficient Toronto," *Globe and Mail*, 26 October 1974.

4. "Wonder Merchants: Modernist Poetry in Vancouver during the

1960s," *Godawful Streets of Man, Open Letter* 3, no. 6 (Winter 1976–77): 191.

5. Dudek, "Literature in English," *Selected Essays and Criticism* (Ottawa: Tecumseh Press, 1978), p. 233.

6. Geddes, "Souster, Rooted and Faithful."

7. Robert Fulford, "The Poet Laureate of the Toronto Streets Looks Sadly Backward," *Toronto Star,* 7 October 1972, p. 65.

8. Gary Geddes and Phyllis Bruce, eds., *15 Canadian Poets* (Toronto: Oxford University Press, 1970), p. 292.

9. Ibid.

10. "The Poet Laureate of the Toronto Streets," p. 65.

11. The Marxist approach I use here is based on Karl Marx's analysis of commodity relationships in *Das Kapital* and is a modification of various theories of nonreferential poetry proposed by Ron Silliman (see "For Open Letter," *Open Letter* 3, no. 7: 89–93) and Steve McCaffery (see "The Death of the Subject," *Open Letter* 3, no. 7: 61–77).

12. "Poetry of the Sixties," *Canadian Literature* 41 (Summer 1969). Reprinted in *Selected Essays and Criticism*, p. 272.

13. "Poetry of the Sixties," *Selected Essays and Criticism*, p. 273.

14. *15 Canadian Poets*, p. 291.

15. "Five Poets" (revision of *Unit of Five*, ed. Ronald Hambleton), *First Statement* 2, no. 11. Reprinted in *Essays, Controversies and Poems*, ed. Miriam Waddington (Toronto: McClelland & Stewart, 1972), p. 40.

Chapter Seven

1. Letter from Cid Corman to Souster, 19 October 1955; ms. in collection of Lakehead University Library.

2. Ms. in collection of Lakehead University Library.

3. In Michael Gnarowski, ed., *Contact 1952–54: Notes on the History and Background of the Periodical and an Index* (Montreal: Delta Canada, 1966), p. 1.

4. "To Souster from Vermont," *Tamarack Review* 34 (Winter 1965): 81–95.

5. "Souster's Vision of Life So Consistent," *Globe and Mail*, 6 December 1975.

6. Letter to Souster, 14 March 1953; ms. in collection of Lakehead University Library.

7. Letter to Souster, 19 October 1955; ms. in collection of Lakehead University Library.

8. Letter to Souster, 14 June 1956; ms. in collection of Lakehead University Library.

9. Letter to Souster, 9 October 1958; ms. in collection of Lakehead University Library.

10. Letter to Souster, 31 August 1962; ms. in collection of Lakehead University Library.

11. Letter to Souster, 30 April 1964; ms. in collection of Lakehead University Library.

12. Letter to Corman, 16 March 1954; ms. in collection of the Humanities Research Center, University of Texas at Austin.

13. Letter to Corman, 10 September 1962; ms. in collection of the Humanities Research Center, University of Texas at Austin.

14. Letter to Corman, 17 May 1970; ms. in collection of the Harriet Irving Library, University of New Brunswick.

15. Letters to Corman; mss. in collection of the Harriet Irving Library, University of New Brunswick.

Chapter Eight

1. "A Rejected Preface to *New Provinces*, 1936," *Towards a View of Canadian Letters* (Vancouver: University of British Columbia Press, 1973), p. 173.

2. "Academic Literature," *First Statement* 2, no. 8 (August 1944). Reprinted in *Selected Essays and Criticism* (Ottawa: Tecumseh Press, 1978) pp. 1–3.

3. "On the Teaching of Modern Literature," *Beyond Culture* (New York: Viking Press, 1961), p. 9.

4. Ibid., p. 13.

5. *The First Person in Literature* (Toronto: CBC Publications, 1967), p. 45.

6. "Functional Poetry," *Delta* 8: 6.

7. Wilhelm Worringer, *Abstraction and Empathy: A Contribution to the Psychology of Style*, trans. Michael Bullock (New York, 1953), p. 133.

8. T.E. Hulme, *Speculations* (New York, 1924), p. 107.

9. "Functional Poetry," p. 6.

10. "In This Number," *Delta* 3: 32.

11. Michael Darling, "An Interview with Louis Dudek," *Essays on Canadian Writing* 3 (Fall 1975): 13.

12. "Literature in English," in J.M.S. Careless and R. Craig Brown, eds., *The Canadians* (Toronto: Macmillan, 1967), p. 651. Reprinted in *Selected Essays and Criticism*, p. 232.

13. Ortega y Gasset, *The Dehumanization of Art* (Princeton: Princeton University Press, 1948), p. 8.

14. "The Psychology of Literature," paper delivered to the CCTE convention, Saskatoon, August 1974. Included in *Selected Essays and Criticism*, p. 369.

15. Ibid.

16. "Literature of the Sixties," *Canadian Literature* 41 *(Summer* 1969). Reprinted in *Selected Essays and Criticism*, p. 279.

17. "The Psychology of Literature," *Selected Essays and Criticism*, pp. 373-74.

18. "An Interview with Louis Dudek," p. 12.

19. *The Dehumanization of Art*, p. 8.

20. Ibid., p. 11.

21. "A Retrospect," *The Literary Essays of Ezra Pound* (London: Faber & Faber, 1954), p. 4.

Bibliography

I. By Dudek

A. BOOKS OF POETRY

Unit of Five: Louis Dudek, Ronald Hambleton, P.K. Page, Raymond Souster, James Wreford. Edited by Ronald Hambleton. Toronto:Ryerson Press, 1944.

East of the City. Toronto: Ryerson Press, 1946.

The Searching Image. Toronto: Ryerson Press, 1952.

Cerberus by Louis Dudek, Raymond Souster and Irving Layton. Toronto: Contact Press, 1952. Dudek preface reprinted in *The Making of Modern Poetry in Canada*, edited by Louis Dudek and Michael Gnarowski. pp. 144-45. Toronto: Ryerson Press, 1967.

Europe. Toronto: Lacoon (Contact) Press, 1954.

The Transparent Sea. Toronto: Contact Press, 1956.

En México. Toronto: Contact Press, 1958.

Laughing Stalks. Toronto: Contact Press, 1958.

Atlantis. Montreal: Delta Canada, 1967.

Collected Poetry. Montreal: Delta Canada, 1971.

B. OTHER BOOKS

Literature and the Press: A History of Printing, Printed Media and Their Relation to Literature. Toronto: Ryerson Press and

Contact Press, 1960. Revision of doctoral thesis completed at Columbia and published by University Microfilms, Ann Arbor, Mich., 1955.

The First Person in Literature. Toronto: CBC Publications, 1967. Texts of six talks for CBC Radio.

Epigrams. Montreal: DC Books, 1975.

Selected Essays and Criticism. Ottawa: Tecumseh Press, 1978.

Technology and Culture. Ottawa: The Golden Dog Press, 1979.

C. WORKS EDITED

Canadian Poems, 1850–1952. Edited by Louis Dudek and Irving Layton. Toronto: Contact Press, 1952.

The Selected Poems by Raymond Souster. Edited and chosen by Louis Dudek. Toronto: Contact Press, 1956.

Delta: A Magazine of Poetry and Criticism. Nos. 1–26. Montreal, October 1957 to October 1966.

Montreal: Paris of America. Edited by Michel Regnier and Louis Dudek. Toronto: Ryerson Press; Montreal: Editions du Jour, 1961.

Poetry of Our Time: An Introduction to Twentieth-Century Poetry Including Modern Canadian Poetry. Toronto: Macmillan, 1965.

The Making of Modern Poetry in Canada: Essential Articles on Contemporary Poetry in English. Edited by Louis Dudek and Michael Gnarowski. Toronto: Ryerson Press, 1967.

All Kinds of Everything: Worlds of Poetry. Toronto: Clarke Irwin, 1973.

D/k: Some Letters of Ezra Pound. Montreal: DC Books, 1974. With notes by Dudek, including the script of the CBC broadcast, "The Letters of Ezra Pound," 14 September 1957.

D. UNCOLLECTED NOTES, ARTICLES AND ADDRESSES

"Geography, Politics and Poetry." *First Statement* 1, no. 16 (April 1943): 2–3.

"A Visit to Ezra Pound." *Contemporary Verse* 32 (Summer 1950): 20–23.

"Poetry and Politics: Or Why It Pays to Be Aesthetic." *Delta* 5 (October 1958): 6.

"T.S. Eliot." In *Architects of Modern Thought*, pp. 137–50. 5th and 6th series. Toronto: CBC Publications, 1962.

"A.J.M. Smith: Aesthetic Master of Canadian Poetry." *The Montreal Star,* 1 December 1962, p. 13.

"Art, Entertainment, and Religion." *Queen's Quarterly* 70 (Autumn 1963): 413–30.

"Marshall McLuhan Defined." *The Gazette*, 6 August 1966, p. 24.

"McLuhanism in a Nutshell." *The Gazette,* 8 April 1968, p. 28.

"Poetry as a Way of Life." *English Quarterly* 1, no. 1 (Summer 1968): 7–17.

"The Poetry of Reason." *English Quarterly* 3, no. 2 (Summer 1970): 5–14.

"A Letter to the Editors [re *First Statement 1942–1945* by Neil H. Fisher]." *Chien d'Or* 4 (November 1974): 1–3.

E. LETTERS

Contact Press Papers. Thomas Fisher Rare Book Library, University of Toronto. Extensive correspondence from Dudek to Souster and Peter Miller, with their replies.

Earle Birney Papers. Thomas Fisher Rare Book Library, University of Toronto. 35 letters from Dudek to Birney, 1946–1974.

Irving Layton Papers. Concordia University Archives. 46 letters from Dudek to Layton, 1947–1960.

John Sutherland Papers. Concordia University Archives. 11 letters from Dudek to Sutherland, 1950–1951.

Raymond Souster Collection. Lakehead University Library. 89 letters from Dudek to Souster, 1951–1958.

Raymond Souster Papers. Thomas Fisher Rare Book Library, University of Toronto. 8 letters from Dudek to Souster, 1961–1968.

II. About Dudek

Barbour, Douglas. "Poet as Philosopher." *Canadian Literature* 53 (Summer 1972): 18–19. Reprinted in *Poets and Critics,* edited by George Woodcock, pp. 110–22. Toronto: Oxford University Press, 1974.

Darling, Michael. "An Interview with Louis Dudek." *Essays on Canadian Writing* 3 (Fall 1975): 2–14.

Fisher, Neil H. *First Statement 1942–1945: An Assessment and an Index.* Ottawa: The Golden Dog Press, 1974.

Francis, Wynne. "A Critic of Life: Louis Dudek as a Man of Letters." *Canadian Literature* 22 (Autumn 1964): 5–23.

————. "Literary Underground: Little Magazines in Canada." *Canadian Literature* 34 (Autumn 1967): 63–70.

————. "The Little Magazine/Small Press Movement since 1950." *Laurentian University Review* 10, no. 2 (February 1978): 89–109.

————. "Montreal Poets of the Forties." *Canadian Literature* 14 (Autumn 1962): 21–34.

Frye, Northrop. Review of *En México* and *Laughing Stalks*. *University of Toronto Quarterly* 28 (July 1959): 354–56.

Gnarowski, Michael. *Contact 1952–1954: Notes on the History and Background of the Periodical and an Index.* Montreal: Delta Canada, 1966.

————. *Contact Press, 1952–1967: A Note on Its Origins and a Check List of Titles.* Montreal: Delta Canada, 1971.

————. *Index to CIV/n, a Little Magazine Edited by Aileen Collins in Association with Jackie Gallagher, Wanda Staniszewska, Stan Razynski in 1953 and 1954 for a Total of Seven Issues: An Author/Title Index with Select Subject Headings, Arranged and Edited by Michael Gnarowski with an Introductory Note by Louis Dudek.* [Montreal]: n.d.

————. "Louis Dudek: A Note." *Yes* 14 (September 1965): 4–6.

Livesay, Dorothy. "The Sculpture of Poetry." *Canadian Literature* 30 (Autumn 1966): 26–35.

Wenek, Karol W.J. *Louis Dudek: A Check List.* Ottawa: The Golden Dog Press, 1975.

Wilson, Milton. "*Other Canadians* and After." In *Masks of Poetry*, edited by A.J.M. Smith, pp. 123–38. Toronto: McClelland and Stewart, 1962.

III: By Souster

A. Books of Poetry

Unit of Five: Louis Dudek, Ronald Hambleton, P.K. Page, Raymond Souster, James Wreford. Edited by Ronald Hambleton. Toronto: Ryerson Press, 1944.

When We Are Young. Montreal: First Statement Press, 1946.

Go to Sleep, World. Toronto: Ryerson Press, 1947.

City Hall Street. Toronto: Ryerson Press, 1951.

Cerberus by Louis Dudek, Raymond Souster and Irving Layton. Toronto: Contact Press, 1952. Souster preface reprinted in *The Making of Modern Poetry in Canada,* edited by Louis Dudek and Michael Gnarowski, pp. 146-47. Toronto: Ryerson Press, 1967.

Shake Hands with the Hangman. Toronto: Contact Press, 1953.

A Dream That is Dying. Toronto: Contact Press, 1954.

For What Time Slays. Toronto: Contact Press, 1955.

Walking Death. Toronto: Contact Press, 1955.

The Selected Poems. Edited and chosen by Louis Dudek. Toronto: Contact Press, 1956.

Crepe-Hanger's Carnival. Toronto: Contact Press, 1958.

A Local Pride. Toronto: Contact Press, 1962.

Place of Meeting: Poems 1958–1960. Toronto: Gallery Editions, [1962].

At Split Rock Falls. Vermont: American Letters Press, 1963.

The Colour of the Times: Collected Poems. Toronto: Ryerson Press, 1964.

Twelve New Poems. Lanham, Md.,: Goosetree Press, 1964.

Ten Elephants on Yonge Street. Toronto: Ryerson Press, 1965.

As Is. Toronto: Oxford University Press, 1967.

Lost & Found: Uncollected Poems 1945-65. Toronto: Clarke Irwin, 1968.

So Far, So Good: Poems 1938-1968. Ottawa: Oberon Press, 1969.

The Years. Ottawa: Oberon Press, 1971.

Selected Poems. Edited by Michael Maclem. Ottawa: Oberon Press, 1972.

Change-up: New Poems. Ottawa: Oberon Press, 1974.

Double-Header (reprints *As Is* and *Lost & Found*). Ottawa: Oberon Press, 1975.

Rain-check. Ottawa: Oberon Press, 1975.

Extra Innings: New Poems. Ottawa: Oberon Press, 1977.

Hanging In. Ottawa: Oberon Press, 1979.

B. NOVELS

The Winter of Time by Raymond Holmes [pseud.]. New Toronto: Export Publishing Enterprises, 1949.

On Target by John Holmes [pseud.]. Toronto: Village Book Store Press, 1973 [1972].

C. WORKS EDITED

Direction. Edited by Raymond Souster, William Goldberg and David Mullen. Nos. 1-10. Sydney, N.S.; Port aux Basques, Nfld.; Dartmouth, N.S.; Toronto, November 1943 to February 1946.

Enterprise. Nos. 1-6. Toronto, January 1948 to July/August 1948.

Contact. Nos. 1-10. Toronto, January 1952 to March 1954.

Combustion. Nos. 1-15. Toronto, January 1957 to August 1960; January 1966.

Poets 56: Ten Younger English-Canadians. Toronto: Contact Press, 1956.

New Wave Canada: The New Explosion in Canadian Poetry. Toronto: Contact Press, 1966.

Generation Now. Edited by Raymond Souster and Richard Woollatt. Don Mills, Ont.: Longman Canada, 1970.

Made in Canada. Edited by Raymond Souster and Douglas Lochhead. Ottawa: Oberon Press, 1970.

100 Poems of Nineteenth-Century Canada. Edited by Douglas Lochhead and Raymond Souster. Toronto: Macmillan, 1974.

D. LETTERS

Cid Corman Collection. Harriet Irving Library, University of New Brunswick. Includes 27 letters from Souster to Corman, 1961–1973.

Cid Corman Collection. Humanities Research Center, University of Texas at Austin. Includes 82 letters from Souster to Corman.

Contact Press Papers. Thomas Fisher Rare Book Library, University of Toronto. Includes extensive correspondence from Souster to Dudek and Peter Miller, with their replies.

Irving Layton Collection. Concordia University Archives.

IV. About Souster

Campbell, Robert. "A Study of the History and Development of Raymond Souster's 'Direction,' 'Contact' and 'Combustion.'" Master's thesis, University of New Brunswick, 1969.

Carruth, Hayden. "To Souster from Vermont." *Tamarack Review* 34 (Winter 1965): 81–95.

Dudek, Louis. "Groundhog among the Stars: The Poetry of Raymond Souster." *Canadian Literature* 22 (Autumn 1964): 34–49.

Fisher, Neil H. *First Statement 1942-1945: An Assessment and an Index.* Ottawa: The Golden Dog Press, 1974.

Francis, Wynne. "Literary Underground: Little Magazines in Canada." *Canadian Literature* 34 (Autumn 1967): 63–70.

Fulford, Robert. "On Raymond Souster: A Good Toronto Poet Toronto Never Discovered." *Maclean's* 77 (18 April 1964): 59. Reprinted in *The Making of Modern Poetry in Canada*, edited by Louis Dudek and Michael Gnarowski, pp. 245–46. Toronto: Ryerson Press, 1967.

Geddes, Gary. "A Cursed and Singular Blessing." *Canadian Literature* 54 (Autumn 1972): 27–36.

Gnarowski, Michael. *Contact 1952-1954: Notes on the History and Background of the Periodical and an Index.* Montreal: Delta Canada, 1966.

_____. *Contact Press, 1952-1967: A Note on Its Origins and a Check List of Titles.* Montreal: Delta Canada, 1971.

————. *An Index to "Direction."* Montreal: Culture, 1965. First published in *Culture* 25 (1964): 405-16.

"The Private World of Raymond Souster." *Time* (Canada edition), 12 June 1964. Reprinted in *The Making of Modern Poetry in Canada*, pp. 241-42.

Wilson, Milton. *"Other Canadians and After."* In *Masks of Poetry,* edited by A.J.M. Smith, pp. 123-38. Toronto: McClelland and Stewart, 1962.

Acknowledgements

The author and the publisher thank the following people and institutions for their generous co-operation in allowing the quotation of various materials: Louis Dudek, for extracts from his poetry, criticism and letters; Raymond Souster, for extracts from his letters; Cid Corman, for extracts from his letters; Peter Miller, for extracts from his letters; Oberon Press, for extracts from the poetry of Raymond Souster; The Thomas Fisher Rare Book Library, University of Toronto, for extracts from letters by Louis Dudek, Raymond Souster and Peter Miller; The Library, Lakehead University, for extracts from letters by Louis Dudek and Cid Corman; The Harriet Irving Library, University of New Brunswick, for extracts from letters by Raymond Souster; The Humanities Research Center, University of Texas at Austin, for extracts from letters by Raymond Souster; The Library, Concordia University, for extracts from letters by Raymond Souster and Cid Corman.

STUDIES IN CANADIAN LITERATURE began in 1969 as a series of critical overviews designed to give students and general readers better access to significant Canadian writing. Now under the general editorship of Gary Geddes, it is a continuing forum for analysis of the work of important Canadian authors both established and experimental.

SCL 1
CHARLES G.D. ROBERTS
W.J. Keith

SCL 3
FREDERICK PHILIP GROVE
Douglas O. Spettigue

SCL 4
MORLEY CALLAGHAN
Victor Hoar

SCL 5
HUGH MACLENNAN
George Woodcock

SCL 6
AL PURDY
George Bowering

SCL 8
SINCLAIR ROSS & ERNEST BUCKLER
Robert D. Chambers

SCL 9
MARGARET AVISON
Ernest Redekop

SCL 10
E.J. PRATT
Sandra Djwa

SCL 11
EARLE BIRNEY
Frank Davey

SCL 12
LEONARD COHEN
Stephen Scobie

SCL 13
ROBERT KROETSCH
Peter Thomas

SCL 14
LOUIS DUDEK & RAYMOND SOUSTER
Frank Davey